CHETNA'S
30
MINUTE
indian

QUICK AND EASY
EVERYDAY MEALS

CHETNA'S
30
MINUTE
indian

CHETNA MAKAN

MITCHELL
BEAZLEY

To my amazing kids, Sia & Yuv, without whom
this book would not have been possible.

First published in Great Britain in 2021 by Mitchell Beazley,
an imprint of Octopus Publishing Group Ltd, Carmelite House,
50 Victoria Embankment, London EC4Y 0DZ
www.octopusbooks.co.uk
www.octopusbooksusa.com

An Hachette UK Company
www.hachette.co.uk

Distributed in the US by Hachette Book Group, 1290 Avenue of the Americas,
4th and 5th Floors, New York, NY 10104

Distributed in Canada by Canadian Manda Group, 664 Annette St., Toronto,
Ontario, Canada M6S 2C8

ISBN 978-1-78472-750-5

A CIP catalogue record for this book is available from the British Library.

Printed and bound in China.

10 9 8 7 6 5 4 3

Editorial Director: Eleanor Maxfield
Art Director: Juliette Norsworthy
Senior Editor: Leanne Bryan
Copy Editor: Jo Richardson
Designer: Geoff Fennell
Photographer: Nassima Rothacker
Food Stylist: Emily Kydd
Props Stylist: Morag Farquhar
Assistant Production Manager: Lucy Carter

Contents

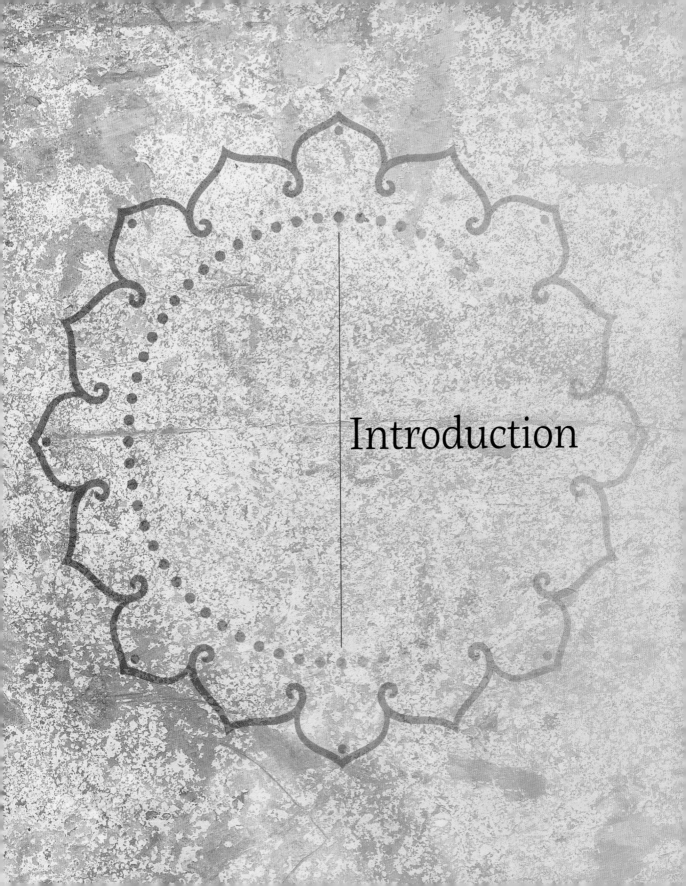

Introduction

A very big hello and a warm welcome to *30-minute Indian*. There are moments when I still can't believe that I am here introducing my new cookbook, and I feel very lucky being able to do something I really love. When I was in school, I was so clear-sighted about my future and totally focused on becoming a fashion designer. I went on to achieve that ambition working in fashion in Mumbai, and was fortunate to have many great opportunities and to enjoy the most amazing few years in the industry. At that time, I had no idea that I would one day be working in a very different sphere, the food industry, and writing my own cookbooks. But in the intervening period, my circumstances changed and I ended up coming to England, where I did various jobs, started a family and made the country my home. I have always been a glass-half-full kind of person and welcomed such a seismic shift in my life with open arms. And now, seven years after I first entered *The Great British Bake Off* tent, I am presenting my fifth cookbook.

The place where I spend the most time is my kitchen. Whether developing new recipes for a book or experimenting with new recipes for my YouTube channel, all my work happens in my kitchen where I have taken over a small part of the dining table as my desk so that I never have to leave the room.

This past year – a strange one for us all – having been homebound with nowhere to go, it felt to me as if that

"I have always tried to work on ideas and recipes that bring something new to the table."

room was the entire world. When the lockdown first happened, I tried to keep busy and shared recipes with my audience every single day. I started getting lots of positive messages from people, saying how much they enjoyed the recipes and how they gave them a little something to look forward to each day, which helped spur me on. I have to admit that it kept me sane by giving me something worthwhile to focus on.

But as days became weeks and weeks became months, I found that people who had relished the whole, sometimes lengthy and involved cooking processes at the outset of lockdown had begun to get bored and give up. Perhaps this was a natural consequence of getting used to lockdown and a slower pace of life, but whatever the situation, day to day, many of us simply don't want to spend ages cooking meals however much we appreciate eating good food.

I have always tried to work on ideas and recipes that bring something new to the table, like the Indian flavour-inspired bakes in my book *The Cardamom Trail* or everyday nutritious Indian meals in *Chetna's Healthy Indian*. So when it came to the concept for this new book, I took into account that recent feedback, along with requests I had received from people who try my recipes all the time. And the message was, yes, we like long recipes that take time and effort with lots of love thrown in, and those are perfect for lazy weekends. But for a meal after a busy day at work, a quick lunch at our desks or on the go, or a snack while watching a film or entertaining friends, what we need are recipes that deliver on ease and speed as well as on flavour. I also wanted to counteract the common perception that Indian food is by nature based on slow-cooked dishes. While there are Indian recipes that take a very long time to make, our everyday food is often fast to prep and cook.

And that's exactly where this book comes in, with its range of delicious Indian dishes that will take no more than 30 minutes of your precious time. It will help you go into the kitchen with confidence and make something full of flavour in a short period of time. But that doesn't mean you can lounge around and still have that plateful ready on cue. Those 30 minutes will be challenging, with lots of chopping, stirring and other activity, but the end will always be in sight when you can sit down and enjoy your meal.

"For a meal after a busy day at work, a quick lunch at our desks or on the go, or a snack while watching a film or entertaining friends, what we need are recipes that deliver on ease and speed as well as on flavour."

I have tried to keep the deliciousness of these recipes intact, specially devising and then repeatedly testing them to cut down on the time involved but not the flavour, and I hope you will see that in the results of your cooking.

There are a few things you need to bear in mind for the recipes to work at their best:

- Before you start, read through the recipe just to get an idea of what's involved.

- The next thing is to get all the pots and pans and other kit you need for the recipe sorted and to hand.

- It's also best to get all the ingredients required assembled and ready to go.

- Don't feel guilty about using canned beans or canned tomatoes, as they will save you hours of cooking time.

- And don't be shy of using ready-peeled ginger and garlic or ready-prepared pastes to save you a few more minutes.

- Where appropriate in the recipes, I have specified using hot stock or water to cut down on time, so use the kettle for boiling water rapidly.

- Most of the cooking processes in these recipes require a relatively high heat, which is good for browning ingredients and thereby bringing out their flavour in less time. Don't be afraid of cooking over a high heat, as you can't leave the kitchen during the half hour anyway, so you might as well make the most of standing in attendance over the hob.

- Be prepared to multitask. I have indicated in the recipes where you can carry out a couple or more steps concurrently, so if the method asks for it, get two pans on the hob, or even three if needed.

- I have timed these recipes to the minute as far as possible, but if you are cooking over a lower heat than advised or cut the veg or meat into bigger pieces than specified, they are likely to take a few extra minutes to cook. On the other hand, you may well be able to speed up the preparation by chopping faster than me or by using a kitchen gadget or having help from a friend or partner.

- In cases where you have more than 30 minutes, feel free to use chicken on rather than off the bone or let dishes slow cook instead of cooking over a higher heat, as I have highlighted in the relevant recipes.

Finally, don't rush the eating part – you have done the hard work and saved yourself time to relax and fully enjoy the flavourful food!

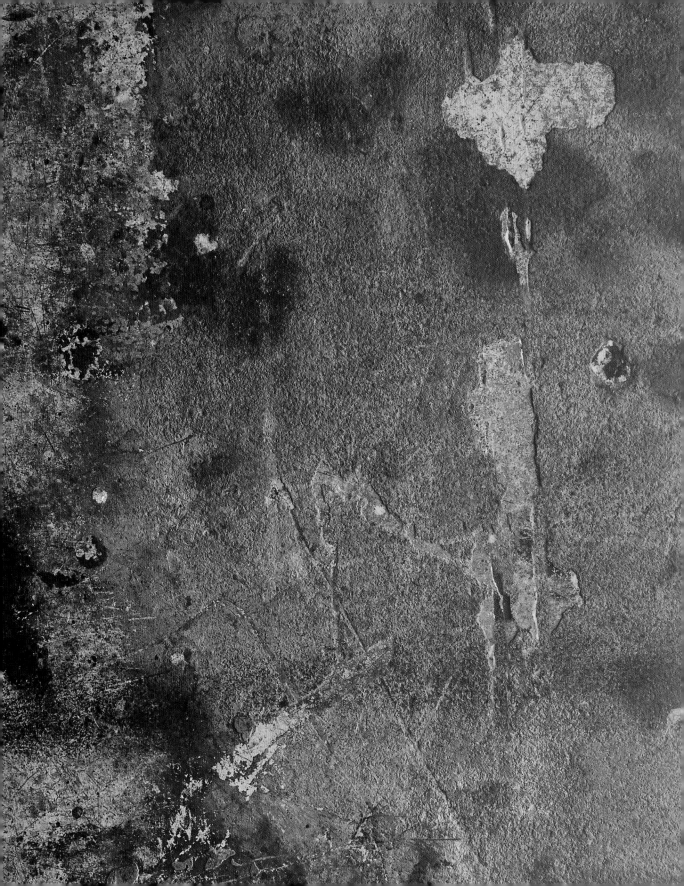

Snacks

Paneer onion masala rolls

Kale, carrot & bean salad

Crispy paneer cubes

Cheesy potato balls

Mango aubergine slices

Sour & spicy potatoes

Masala pastry

Pastry samosa

New potato & peanut salad

Chickpea & courgette parcels

Cheesy bread pakora

Corn pepper cheese sandwich

Masala peanuts

A delicious crispy snack to please the crowds, everyone from grown-ups to kids loves these rolls. This is a very versatile recipe, so once you have cooked up this version, you can try different chutneys with the paneer filling or mix up different variations that you like. Although the rolls are best served warm, believe me no one will complain if you serve them at room temperature.

Paneer onion masala rolls

Paneer pyaaz masala papdi

MAKES 18

1 sheet of ready-rolled puff pastry, 320g (11¼oz)

plain flour, for dusting

5–6 tablespoons Coriander Peanut Chutney (see page 162)

1 egg, lightly beaten, for glazing

FOR THE FILLING

225g (8oz) paneer, grated

1 red onion, finely chopped

1 green chilli, finely chopped

1 teaspoon salt

1 teaspoon amchur (mango powder)

1 teaspoon chilli powder

20g (¾oz) fresh coriander leaves, finely chopped

Preheat the oven to 200°C (400°F), Gas Mark 6.

Mix all the filling ingredients together in a bowl until well combined.

Unroll the pastry sheet on a lightly floured work surface and spread all over with the chutney. Spread the filling mixture on top as evenly as possible, then use your fingers to lightly press the mixture on to the pastry.

Starting from one longer side, roll up the pastry into a log. Brush all over with the beaten egg and slice it into 18 pieces about 1.5cm (⅝ inch) thick.

Place on a baking sheet and bake for 20–25 minutes until crispy and golden. Serve warm.

All the different textures and flavours from the kale, carrots, beans and cashew nuts come together really well here with the addition of a little spice. This is one of those recipes that you can serve warm with rice and dal, such as Courgette Moong Dal with Tomato Tempering (see page 118) or Sweet and Sour Lentils (see page 112), or at room temperature as a salad with some bread, and also as part of a barbecue spread.

Kale, carrot & bean salad

Kale, gajar, sem salad

SERVES 4

2 tablespoons sunflower oil

1 teaspoon black mustard seeds

2 red onions, thinly sliced

200g (7oz) cavolo nero, finely chopped

2 carrots, cut into matchsticks

¾ teaspoon salt

1 teaspoon chilli powder

1 teaspoon chaat masala

1 tomato, thinly sliced

400g (14oz) can adzuki beans, drained and rinsed

15–20 cashew nuts

juice of 1 lime

Heat the oil in a pan and add the mustard seeds. Once they start to sizzle, add the onions and cook over a medium to low heat for 5 minutes until they start to soften.

Stir in the cavolo nero, carrots, salt and ground spices, then cover and cook over a medium to low heat for 8 minutes.

Add the tomato, beans and cashew nuts and mix well, then cover again and cook over a medium to low heat for another 8 minutes.

Add the lime juice and mix well, then serve.

Snack, light meal, side or starter – I don't know how to categorize this dish. In India, you would serve it as a snack with some chai or even as a starter, however heavy the meal to follow (there is always room for fried paneer). The spiced yogurt is a great marinade, with the addition of gram flour ensuring that it sticks to the paneer. Toasting the flour is important, as it eliminates the raw taste, resulting in a delicious and crisp paneer. Serve with Coriander Peanut Chutney (see page 162).

Crispy paneer cubes

SERVES 2

2 tablespoons gram flour (besan/chickpea flour)

70ml (2½fl oz) natural yogurt

¼ teaspoon salt

1 teaspoon kashmiri chilli powder

1 teaspoon kasuri methi (dried fenugreek leaves)

½ teaspoon amchur (mango powder)

½ teaspoon garam masala

½ teaspoon ground cumin

200g (7oz) paneer, cut into 2.5cm (1 inch) cubes

sunflower oil, for shallow-frying

Heat a frying pan, add the flour and toast over a low heat for about 2 minutes until it starts to change colour, stirring constantly.

Put the toasted flour into a bowl with the yogurt, salt and spices and mix together well. Add the paneer cubes and gently turn in the marinade until well coated.

Heat enough oil for shallow-frying in a frying pan. Carefully add the paneer to the hot oil and cook over a medium to high heat for 1–2 minutes, turning halfway through, until golden and crispy. Serve warm.

This widely loved snack in India, which is famed in Mumbai as batata vada, is customarily sold in a soft bun with a garlic and chilli chutney. Its popularity has spread and it's now available in many Indian restaurants worldwide. Where I come from, these delicious potato balls are called alu banda and are sold in small shops and street stalls in the mornings for breakfast with chai. So why not serve this with some Coriander Peanut Chutney (see page 162) and piping hot masala chai?

Cheesy potato balls

Cheesy alu banda

MAKES 8

2 potatoes, peeled and cut into 1cm (½ inch) pieces

1 tablespoon sunflower oil, plus extra for deep-frying

1 green chilli, finely chopped

10 fresh curry leaves, finely chopped

½ teaspoon black mustard seeds

½ teaspoon salt

½ teaspoon chilli powder

½ teaspoon ground turmeric

1 tablespoon water

30g (1oz) Cheddar cheese, cut into small cubes

FOR THE BATTER

100g (3½oz) gram flour (besan/chickpea flour)

½ teaspoon salt

½ teaspoon chilli powder

½ teaspoon ground turmeric

about 120ml (8 tablespoons) water

Put the potato pieces in a pan and cover with water. Bring to the boil and cook for 5 minutes until tender. Drain and set aside.

Heat the 1 tablespoon of oil in a pan and add the green chilli, curry leaves and mustard seeds. Once they start to sizzle, stir in the salt and ground spices and cook over a low heat for a few seconds. Add the measured water and the cooked potatoes and mix well, then leave to cool while you make the batter.

Mix together all the batter ingredients except the water in a bowl. Then gradually whisk in enough of the water to make a smooth batter with a coating consistency.

Divide the potato mixture into 8 portions and form each into a ball about the size of a lime. Push a cube of cheese into the centre of each potato ball and mould the potato mixture back around it to seal it in.

Heat enough oil for deep-frying in a deep-fat fryer or deep, heavy-based pan (ensuring the pan is no more than one-third full) to 180°C (350°F). Line a plate with kitchen paper. Dip one potato ball at a time into the batter and then carefully add to the hot oil. Deep-fry, in small batches, for a minute on each side until golden. Transfer to the paper-lined plate to absorb the excess oil while you fry the remaining balls. Serve warm.

The mighty aubergine is such a gorgeous vegetable and there are so many ways to cook it, with the addition of varying spices making it taste very different. These delicious slices have a lovely sour kick from the amchur (mango powder). A great snack served with a spicy chutney such as Tomato and Tamarind Chutney (see page 166), it also makes a great side along with some dal and rice.

Mango aubergine slices

Amchur baigan tukde

SERVES 2

1 aubergine, cut into slices 5mm (¼ inch) thick

40g (1½oz) rice flour

40g (1½oz) gram flour (besan/chickpea flour)

¼ teaspoon salt

sunflower oil, for shallow-frying

FOR THE SPICE MIX

1 teaspoon amchur (mango powder)

1 teaspoon ground coriander

½ teaspoon chilli powder

½ teaspoon ground turmeric

½ teaspoon salt

Mix all the spice mix ingredients together in a bowl. Place the aubergine slices on a plate, sprinkle over half the spice mix and rub it into the aubergine with your fingertips. Turn the slices over, sprinkle over the remaining spice mix and rub in as before. Let the aubergine rest for 5 minutes.

Meanwhile, mix the rice flour, gram flour and salt together in another bowl.

Heat enough oil for shallow-frying in a frying pan. Line a plate with kitchen paper.

Coat the aubergine slices in the flour mixture, add to the hot oil and cook over a medium to low heat for 1–2 minutes on each side until golden and cooked through. Transfer to the paper-lined plate to absorb the excess oil, then serve.

Chaat is the ultimate Indian street food, and something that many people are now familiar with. This potato version is slightly sour and spicy from the two chutneys – my favourites – that I've added to it. I always have a jar of the ginger and chilli chutney in the refrigerator, as it keeps for up to a couple of weeks, and while the coriander chutney lasts only a few days in the refrigerator, it takes only minutes to make. Serve this in a big dish for sharing or in individual bowls.

Sour & spicy potatoes

Alu chaat

SERVES 4

4 potatoes, about 1kg (2lb 4oz) in total, peeled and cut into 2.5cm (1 inch) pieces

4 tablespoons Coriander Peanut Chutney (see page 162)

100ml (3½fl oz) natural yogurt, lightly whisked

pinch of chilli powder

2 tablespoons Ginger and Chilli Chutney (see page 158)

¼ teaspoon chaat masala

2–3 tablespoons fine sev

handful of fresh pomegranate seeds

salt

Put the potato pieces in a pan, cover with water and add 1 teaspoon of salt. Bring to the boil, then cook for 5–7 minutes until cooked through. Drain and let them cool for 5 minutes.

Place the potatoes in a bowl with 2 tablespoons of the coriander peanut chutney and mix well. Transfer to a serving bowl and drizzle the yogurt on top. Then sprinkle with a pinch of salt and the chilli powder.

Drizzle the remaining coriander peanut chutney and all the ginger and chilli chutney on top, followed by the chaat masala and then the sev. Sprinkle over the pomegranate seeds and serve immediately.

This is the most popular snack in my house. It used to be my favourite snack growing up and now it's my kids' favourite, too. My mum would always keep a box of papdi in the cupboard and refill it as soon as it was empty. I make them often but not as often as she did, as I find they disappear faster than I can make them. No one can ever have just one.

Masala pastry

Masala papdi

MAKES 1 PLATEFUL

100g (3½oz) plain flour, plus extra for dusting

1 tablespoon kasuri methi (dried fenugreek leaves)

¼ teaspoon salt

¼ teaspoon carom seeds

¼ teaspoon garam masala

¼ teaspoon chilli powder

¼ teaspoon ground turmeric

1 tablespoon sunflower oil, plus extra for deep-frying

about 45ml (3 tablespoons) water

Mix all the dry ingredients together in a bowl. Add the 1 tablespoon of oil and rub in with your fingertips until the mixture resembles breadcrumbs. Then gradually add just enough of the water, or a little more if needed, to bring the mixture together into a soft dough. Cover and let it rest for 5 minutes.

Divide the dough into 4 portions. Roll out each portion on a lightly floured work surface into a thin sheet about 15–18cm (6–7 inches) square. Using a sharp knife, cut the sheet into strips about 2.5cm (1 inch) wide.

Heat enough oil for deep-frying in a deep-fat fryer or deep, heavy-based pan (ensuring the pan is no more than one-third full) to about 170°C (340°F). Line a plate with kitchen paper.

Deep-fry the pastry strips, in batches, for a few seconds, then turn over and cook until golden. Transfer to the paper-lined plate to absorb the excess oil and cool while you fry the remaining pastry strips. They will crisp up as they cool down.

The Masala Pastry will keep in an airtight container for up to 2 weeks.

If making samosas is something that scares you a little or you find it a bit tricky, then these pastry samosas are ideal. While the filling is the traditional one, I have used ready-rolled pastry to save time and effort. I tried deep-frying these, but everyone in my family preferred them baked, as they came out flaky and beautiful.

Pastry samosa

Papdi samosa

MAKES 18

2 potatoes, peeled and cut into 1cm (½ inch) pieces

100g (3½oz) frozen peas

½ teaspoon salt

½ teaspoon chilli powder

½ teaspoon chaat masala

1 sheet of ready-rolled shortcrust pastry, 320g (11½oz)

plain flour, for dusting

1 egg, beaten, for glazing

Preheat the oven to 200°C (400°F), Gas Mark 6.

Put the potatoes in a pan, cover with water and bring to the boil, then cook for 5 minutes until cooked through. Add the peas and cook for a minute.

Drain the vegetables, transfer to a wide pan and let them cool for a couple of minutes. Then add the salt, chilli powder and chaat masala and mash the mixture with a potato masher.

Unroll the pastry on a lightly floured work surface and cut in half lengthways. Divide the potato mixture in half and spoon each portion along one long side of each pastry rectangle, as if making sausage rolls. Brush the pastry edges with beaten egg and roll up into a long cylinder. Brush all over with beaten egg.

Cut each cylinder into 9 lengths and place on a baking sheet. Bake for 15 minutes until golden. Serve warm.

For me, salads should have some body and bite to them, and work well as a side or a starter. This recipe is just that, since although I am calling it a salad, you could equally class it as a sabji. The fresh herbs, spices, onions and peanuts all add to the layers of flavour, with the nuts also contributing crunch. To save time here, I've used ready-roasted peanuts – the ones sold in the snack aisle, which are slightly salted, are fine to use.

New potato & peanut salad

Alu & moongphalli salad

SERVES 4

500g (1lb 2oz) new potatoes, cut into quarters

2 tablespoons sunflower oil

FOR THE DRESSING

2 tablespoons sunflower oil

1 teaspoon cumin seeds

1 teaspoon black mustard seeds

10 fresh curry leaves

50g (1¾oz) roasted peanuts, slightly crushed with a pestle and mortar

1 onion, thinly sliced

1 green chilli, finely chopped

½ teaspoon salt

1 teaspoon chaat masala

handful of fresh coriander leaves

handful of fresh mint leaves

Preheat the oven to 200°C (400°F), Gas Mark 6.

Put the potato pieces in a pan, cover with water and bring to the boil, then cook for 5 minutes. Drain.

Heat the oil in a baking tray in the oven for a minute. Add the drained potato to the hot oil, toss until well coated and roast for 12–15 minutes until cooked through and golden.

Meanwhile, to make the dressing, heat the oil in a pan and add the cumin and mustard seeds. Once they start to sizzle, add the curry leaves and peanuts and cook over a medium to low heat for a minute. Then add the onion and green chilli and cook for 5 minutes until they have softened. Stir in the salt and chaat masala, then take the pan off the heat.

Add the roasted potatoes and herbs to the pan and mix together until well combined. Serve warm or at room temperature.

These parcels are perfect when you want a quick snack or something to take on a picnic, or have friends coming over. These are little pockets of joy, as they taste fantastic and no one would believe how easy they are to put together.

Chickpea & courgette parcels

Chana potli

MAKES 8

2 tablespoons sunflower oil

1 small onion, finely chopped

1 green chilli, finely chopped

1 small courgette, finely chopped

½ teaspoon salt

½ teaspoon chilli powder

½ teaspoon garam masala

1 tablespoon Coriander Peanut Chutney (see page 162)

400g (14oz) can chickpeas, drained and rinsed

plain flour, for dusting

1 sheet of ready-rolled puff pastry, 320g (11½oz)

1 egg, lightly beaten, for glazing

Preheat the oven to 200°C (400°F), Gas Mark 6.

Heat the oil in a pan, add the onion and green chilli and cook over a medium to high heat for 2 minutes until they begin to soften. Then add the courgette and cook for 2 minutes.

Stir in the salt, spices, chutney and chickpeas and cook over a high heat for a minute. Immediately transfer to a large plate to cool down slightly.

Unroll the pastry sheet on a lightly floured work surface and cut it into 8 equal rectangles. Place a spoonful of the chickpea mixture on one side of each pastry rectangle and fold over the other side to enclose. Press the edges of each parcel together with a fork to seal, then brush with the beaten egg.

Place on a baking sheet and bake for 15 minutes until golden and crispy. Serve warm.

Bread pakora are a popular Indian street food and there are so many variations out there. They are also often made at home as a snack and I like to cook these up for a lazy lunch. You can enjoy them as sandwiches or cut them up and serve as bite-sized snacks. Either way, they're great with a chutney such as Coriander Peanut Chutney (see page 162) or even some ketchup.

Cheesy bread pakora

MAKES 2

4 slices of white bread

2 tablespoons salted butter

4 tablespoons grated Cheddar cheese

2 tablespoons sunflower oil

FOR THE POTATO MIXTURE

1 large potato, peeled and cut into 1cm (½ inch) pieces

1 tablespoon sunflower oil

10 fresh curry leaves

2.5cm (1 inch) piece of fresh root ginger, peeled and grated

2 garlic cloves, grated

1 teaspoon garam masala

1 teaspoon amchur (mango powder)

½ teaspoon chilli powder

½ teaspoon salt

handful of fresh coriander leaves, finely chopped

FOR THE BATTER

100g (3½oz) gram flour (besan/chickpea flour)

½ teaspoon salt

½ teaspoon chilli powder

½ teaspoon ground turmeric

½ teaspoon carom seeds

about 130ml (4¼fl oz) water

To make the potato mixture, put the potato pieces in a pan, cover with water and bring to the boil, then cook for 5 minutes. Drain and mash with a fork.

Heat the oil in another pan, add the curry leaves, ginger and garlic and cook over a low heat for a few seconds. Then add all the spices, salt, coriander and mashed potato and mix together well. Take the pan off the heat and let the mixture cool slightly. Then either use your hands or a potato masher to press the mixture together.

To make the batter, mix the gram flour, salt and spices together in a bowl. Then gradually whisk in enough of the measured water to make a smooth batter with a coating consistency.

Spread one side of each bread slice with the butter. Divide the potato mixture between 2 of the buttered bread slices and spread over, then sprinkle each with 2 tablespoons cheese. Cover with the other bread slices, buttered side down, and press to seal. You can tidy up the sandwiches by cutting off the crusts if you wish, or leave them as they are.

Heat the oil in a frying pan. Carefully dip one sandwich at a time into the batter, add to the hot oil and cook over a high to medium heat for 1–2 minutes on each side until nice and golden. Serve the sandwiches immediately, either whole or cut into quarters.

Crispy on the outside, the flavours of green pepper, spring onion, sweetcorn and cheese work so well together for the filling. This is one of those snacks that would make a great lunch or dinner, or even a canapé. Enjoy it with salad in summer or with some soup in winter, or just on its own. You can use any kind of bread – sliced, seeded, homemade or even a wrap.

Corn pepper cheese sandwich

Makka shimla mirch sandwich

MAKES 4

100g (3½oz) frozen sweetcorn kernels

1 green pepper, cored, deseeded and finely chopped

4 spring onions, finely chopped

1 green chilli, finely chopped

150g (5½oz) Cheddar cheese, grated

2 teaspoons chilli garlic sauce

pinch of ground black pepper

8 slices of sourdough

salted butter, for spreading

Cook the sweetcorn in a pan of boiling water for 2 minutes, then drain and let it cool for 2 minutes.

Transfer the sweetcorn to a bowl, add the green pepper, spring onions, chilli, cheese, sauce and black pepper and mix together well.

Spread one side of each bread slice with some butter. Place 4 slices, buttered side down, in a griddle pan or heavy-based frying pan. Spread one-quarter of the cheese mixture over each bread slice, then cover with the other bread slices, buttered side up. Cook over a medium heat for 1–2 minutes on each side until crispy and golden. Serve warm.

These crispy, spicy and delicious peanuts are a very popular snack in India, where you will find them in all corner shops and sweet shops. They are so easy to make at home, and perfect with a cup of tea or a drink. The only problem is that once you start eating them, it's quite difficult to stop!

Masala peanuts

Masala moongphalli

MAKES 1 LARGE BOWLFUL

60g (2¼oz) gram flour (besan/chickpea flour)

30g (1oz) rice flour

20g (¾oz) cornflour

1 teaspoon chilli powder

½ teaspoon ground turmeric

½ teaspoon garlic salt

250g (9oz) roasted, unsalted peanuts

2 teaspoons sunflower oil, plus extra for shallow-frying

60ml (4 tablespoons) water

Mix all the flours and spices together in a bowl, then stir in the peanuts.

Add the 2 teaspoons of oil and mix well, then gradually whisk in the water to make a thick gloopy batter that coats the peanuts.

Heat enough oil for shallow-frying in a frying pan. Line a plate with kitchen paper.

Working in a couple of batches, carefully add the coated peanuts to the hot oil, separating them as you go if you can, and cook over a medium heat for 2–3 minutes until golden and crispy. Transfer to the paper-lined plate to absorb the excess oil and cool while you fry the remaining peanuts. They will crisp up more once they have cooled down.

The peanuts will keep in an airtight container for up to 2 weeks.

Fish & Seafood

Coconut curry leaf prawns

Salmon curry

Sea bass with curry sauce

Peanut haddock curry

Crab curry

Squid & mangetout curry

Amritsar-style fish

Spicy tomato & prawn curry

Fish & lentil curry

If you are looking for a quick starter or a snack to share, then these crispy prawns are just perfect. With simple seasoning, the prawns take up the lovely flavour from the curry leaves and the coconut, making them delicately moreish. In all honesty, these are divine on their own, but of course if you have a delicious chutney in the refrigerator, such as the Ginger and Chilli Chutney (see page 158), do serve it as an accompaniment.

Coconut curry leaf prawns

Nariyal curry patta zhinga

MAKES 8

30g (1oz) plain flour
pinch of salt
pinch of ground black pepper
1 egg
30g (1oz) desiccated coconut
1 garlic clove, grated
¼ teaspoon salt
¼ teaspoon chilli powder
10 fresh curry leaves, finely chopped
8 uncooked prawns, peeled and deveined, tails left intact
sunflower oil, for shallow-frying

Mix the flour, salt and pepper together in a bowl.

Break the egg into a second bowl and beat lightly.

In a third bowl, combine the coconut, garlic, salt, chilli powder and curry leaves.

Dip one prawn at a time into the seasoned flour, coating it well, then into the egg, making sure it is fully covered, and finally into the coconut mixture until coated all over.

Heat enough oil for shallow-frying in a frying pan over a medium heat. Once hot, carefully add all the prawns to the hot oil and cook for 1–2 minutes on each side until beautifully golden and crispy, then serve.

Fish is not just quick and easy to cook but you can also add lovely flavours to the curry that can be readily soaked up by it. In this case, I have kept the spices simple, with ground coriander leading the pack. The broccoli is the perfect addition, bringing bite and colour to the dish. Serve with Spinach Onion Pulao (see page 145) or some plain rice.

Salmon curry

SERVES 4

2 tablespoons sunflower oil

1 teaspoon black mustard seeds

2 onions, finely chopped

1 green chilli, finely chopped

2 garlic cloves, grated

2 tomatoes, finely chopped

1 teaspoon salt

2 teaspoons ground coriander

1 teaspoon chilli powder

1 tablespoon tamarind paste

200ml (7fl oz) boiling water

200g (7oz) Tenderstem broccoli, cut in half

FOR THE SALMON

2 tablespoons sunflower oil

600g (1lb 5oz) skinless salmon fillets, cut into 5–7.5cm (2–3 inch) pieces

pinch of salt

pinch of ground black pepper

Heat the oil in a pan and add the mustard seeds. Once they start to sizzle, add the onions with the green chilli and cook over a medium heat for 8 minutes until golden. Then add the garlic and cook for a minute.

Stir in the tomatoes and cook over a medium heat for 8 minutes until soft and mushy.

Meanwhile, heat a frying pan and add the oil for the salmon. Once hot, sprinkle the salmon with the salt and pepper and cook over a medium heat for 2 minutes, turning halfway through, until golden. Transfer to a plate.

Add the salt, ground spices and tamarind paste to the tomato mixture and mix well. Then pour in the measured boiling water and stir in the broccoli. Cover and cook over a medium heat for 5 minutes.

Add the salmon pieces to the curry and cook for 2 minutes, then serve.

Slightly similar to katsu curry, I started making this at home using nice fresh fish and my own variation of the popular curry sauce. This is so light and fragrant that you can serve it with some chicken or lots of roasted vegetables. Otherwise, enjoy it just with steamed greens, or a mixed salad of cucumber ribbons, chopped cherry tomatoes, thinly sliced red onion and mint and coriander leaves as pictured overleaf.

Sea bass with curry sauce

SERVES 2

lime slices and/or wedges, to serve

FOR THE CURRY SAUCE

2 tablespoons sunflower oil

1 onion, roughly chopped

2 green chillies, roughly chopped

1 tablespoon curry powder

1 teaspoon plain flour

200–250ml (7–9fl oz) whole milk

½ teaspoon salt

¼ teaspoon ground black pepper

FOR THE FISH

2 sea bass fillets, skin on

pinch of salt

pinch of ground turmeric

1 tablespoon sunflower oil

1 tablespoon salted butter

To make the curry sauce, heat the oil in a pan, add the onion and cook over a medium to low heat for 5 minutes until it begins to soften. Add the green chillies and cook for a minute.

Mix in the curry powder and flour and cook, stirring, for a few seconds. Then gradually add 200ml (7fl oz) of the milk, stirring constantly, and cook for a couple of minutes until the mixture thickens.

Blitz the mixture with a hand blender or in a blender or food processor until smooth. Return to the pan, if necessary, and add the salt and pepper. If the sauce is too thick, add the extra 50ml (2fl oz) milk and mix well. Keep warm while you cook the fish.

Wash the fish fillets and pat them dry, then sprinkle with the salt and turmeric. Heat the oil and butter in a frying pan, add the fish skin-side down and cook over a medium to high heat for 3–4 minutes until the skin is nice and crispy, then carefully turn over and cook the flesh side for a minute.

Place the fish fillets skin-side up on serving plates and pour around the sauce. Serve immediately with some lime slices and/or wedges.

A delicious fish curry, enriched with a warm nutty flavour, you really do have to try this to understand its distinctive qualities. It's beautiful with some rice, or serve with bread such as the Tandoori Masala Roti (see page 128) to mop up all that deliciousness.

Peanut haddock curry

Moongphalli machali

SERVES 4

500g (1lb 2oz) skinless haddock fillet, cut into 5cm (2 inch) pieces

pinch of salt

pinch of ground turmeric

1 tablespoon lemon juice

FOR THE CURRY

2 tablespoons sunflower oil

1 bay leaf

2 cardamom pods

1 cinnamon stick

2 onions, grated

2 tomatoes, grated

200ml (7fl oz) boiling water

½ teaspoon salt

FOR THE PASTE

1 tablespoon sunflower oil

50g (1¾oz) roasted, unsalted peanuts, plus extra to garnish

2 garlic cloves, roughly chopped

2.5cm (1 inch) piece of fresh root ginger, peeled and roughly chopped

4 red chillies, roughly chopped

100ml (3½fl oz) water

Place the fish pieces on a plate, sprinkle with the salt and turmeric and drizzle with the lemon juice, then rub the seasonings in well with your fingertips. Let the fish rest while you prepare the curry.

Heat the oil in a pan, add the whole spices and then the onions and cook over a medium heat for 8 minutes until golden.

Add the tomatoes and cook for 8 minutes until soft and mushy.

Meanwhile, to make the paste, heat a small pan and add the oil. Once hot, add the peanuts and cook over a low heat for a minute until golden. Then add the garlic, ginger and chillies and cook for a minute. Pour in the measured water and mix well. Then blitz the mixture to a paste in a blender (preferably) or a food processor.

Add the paste to the tomato mixture with the measured boiling water and salt and bring to the boil. Place the fish pieces in the curry and gently stir. Cover and cook over a medium heat for 5 minutes until the fish is just cooked and flaky, then serve, garnished with chopped peanuts.

Fennel, cumin and mustard make a lovely combination of spice seeds, and one that does most of the work in this recipe. The delicious crab meat soaks up all the flavours and goes really well with the coconut milk. Serve with Spiced Layered Flatbread (see page 135) or some rice.

Crab curry

Kekada curry

SERVES 4

2 tablespoons sunflower oil

1 teaspoon fennel seeds

1 teaspoon cumin seeds

1 teaspoon black mustard seeds

6–8 fresh curry leaves

1 onion, finely chopped

2 garlic cloves, grated

2.5cm (1 inch) piece of fresh root ginger, peeled and grated

400ml (14oz) can coconut milk

½ teaspoon salt

1 teaspoon ground turmeric

1 teaspoon chilli powder

1 teaspoon ground coriander

100ml (3½fl oz) water, if needed

400g (14oz) white crab meat

20g (¾oz) fresh coriander leaves, finely chopped

juice of 1 lemon

Heat the oil in a pan, add the fennel, cumin and mustard seeds and let them sizzle for a few seconds. Add the curry leaves followed by the onion and cook over a medium heat for 8 minutes until golden. Then add the garlic and ginger and cook for a minute.

Pour in the coconut milk and stir in the salt and ground spices, then cover and cook over a low heat for 5 minutes to bring the flavours together. If you find the consistency too thick, add the measured water.

Stir in the crab meat and chopped coriander, cover again and cook over a low heat for another 5 minutes.

Add the lemon juice and mix well, then serve.

Living by the seaside and very close to a fishmonger makes it very easy for me to get hold of fresh fish. I usually go there and decide what I want to cook after seeing the latest catch. They often have the most beautiful squid and I like to pair that with bright green mangetout in this coconut curry for a pleasing crunch. Serve with some rice.

Squid & mangetout curry

SERVES 2

2 tablespoons sunflower oil

1 teaspoon black mustard seeds

10 fresh curry leaves

1 green chilli, thinly sliced

1 onion, finely chopped

2 garlic cloves, grated

2 tomatoes, finely chopped

40g (1½oz) fresh coconut, grated

200ml (7fl oz) water

¾ teaspoon salt

½ teaspoon chilli powder

½ teaspoon ground turmeric

2 teaspoons ground coriander

400g (14oz) cleaned squid, thinly sliced

80g (3oz) mangetout

Heat the oil in a pan and add the mustard seeds. Once they start to sizzle, add the curry leaves and green chilli followed by the onion and cook over a medium heat for 6 minutes until the onion is softened and lightly golden. Add the garlic and cook for a minute.

Stir in the tomatoes and cook over a medium heat for 2 minutes until they start to soften. Then add the coconut with the measured water, cover and cook over a medium to low heat for 10 minutes until everything is mushy and cooked.

Add the salt and ground spices and mix well. Then add the squid and cook over a medium heat, uncovered, for 2–3 minutes until just cooked.

Stir in the mangetout and cook for a minute longer, then serve.

There are many delicious ways in which fish is cooked in Amritsar in North India, and when I visited the city a few years ago I fell in love with the local food. This recipe is inspired by a dish I ate there in a dhabba (small street-side restaurant), and even though it is simple, it's still so delicious. If you can't find trout, then feel free to use any other firm white fish. This is great served with Coriander Peanut Chutney (see page 162).

Amritsar-style fish

SERVES 4

sunflower oil, for shallow-frying

1 trout, about 400–500g (14oz–1lb 2oz), cleaned, gutted and cut into 8 steaks about 1cm (½ inch) thick

FOR THE BATTER

50g (1¾oz) gram flour (besan/chickpea flour)

35g (1¼oz) plain flour

35g (1¼oz) cornflour

2 garlic cloves, grated

2.5cm (1 inch) piece of fresh root ginger, peeled and grated

1 teaspoon carom seeds

½ teaspoon salt

½ teaspoon chilli powder

½ teaspoon ground turmeric

about 150ml (5fl oz) water

TO SERVE

lime wedges

sliced red onion

chilli flakes

To make the batter, mix together all the ingredients except the measured water in a bowl. Then gradually whisk in enough of the water to make a smooth batter with a coating consistency.

Heat enough oil for shallow-frying in a frying pan. Line a plate with kitchen paper.

Wash the fish pieces and pat them dry. Dip one piece at a time into the batter and then carefully add to the hot oil. Cook over a medium to low heat for 2–3 minutes on each side until golden and cooked through. Transfer to the paper-lined plate to absorb the excess oil.

Serve with lime wedges and sliced red onion, sprinkled with the chilli flakes.

Prawns are so quick to cook and they are great in curries, as they soak up all the flavours and become juicy and delicious. It is almost impossible to go wrong here, with the tomato and onion paste delivering a kick from the dried red chillies and then cooked with spices to create a beautiful sauce for the prawns to swim in. All you need with this is a pile of steaming hot rice or some warm bread – try the Spiced Layered Flatbread (see page 135).

Spicy tomato & prawn curry

Theeki tamatar zingha curry

SERVES 4

FOR THE PASTE

2 onions, roughly chopped

2 garlic cloves, roughly chopped

4 dried red chillies

400g (14oz) can plum tomatoes

FOR THE CURRY

2 tablespoons rapeseed oil

1 teaspoon black mustard seeds

10 fresh curry leaves

½ teaspoon salt

½ teaspoon ground black pepper

1 teaspoon sugar

16 raw prawns, peeled and deveined

Put all the paste ingredients into a blender (preferably) or a food processor and blitz until smooth.

To make the curry, heat the oil in a pan and add the mustard seeds. Once they start to sizzle, add the curry leaves and cook until they start to sizzle, then immediately stir in the paste. Cover and cook over a medium to low heat for 15–20 minutes, stirring halfway through, until the tomato mixture is cooked.

Add the salt, pepper, sugar and the prawns, cover again and cook for 5 minutes until the prawns are cooked, then serve.

Fish in any curry is delicious but when cooked with lentils it makes for a wonderfully creamy and hearty dish. I asked my fishmonger which fish he suggested I cook in this curry and he gave me this lovely hake. It worked a treat, but any other firm white fish fillet would be lovely. Serve with Spinach Onion Pulao (see page 145) or plain rice.

Fish & lentil curry

Machali aur daal

SERVES 4

2 tablespoons rapeseed oil

1 teaspoon black mustard seeds

1 large red onion, finely chopped

2.5cm (1 inch) piece of fresh root ginger, peeled and grated

2 tomatoes, finely chopped

1 teaspoon salt

2 teaspoons curry powder

1 teaspoon ground turmeric

1 teaspoon chilli powder

150g (5½oz) masoor dal (split red lentils)

400ml (14fl oz) can coconut milk

100ml (3½fl oz) boiling water

400g (14oz) skinless hake fillet or any firm white fish, cut into pieces 7.5cm (3 inches) long

chopped chives, to serve

Heat the oil in a pan and add the mustard seeds. Once they start to sizzle, add the onion and cook over a medium heat for 5 minutes until softened and starting to change colour. Then add the ginger and cook for a minute.

Add the tomatoes and cook over a medium heat for 2 minutes until they start to soften.

Stir in the salt and ground spices and then the lentils. Pour in the coconut milk followed by the measured boiling water. Cover and cook over a low to medium heat for 10 minutes until the lentils are soft.

Place the fish pieces in the lentils, cover again and cook over a medium heat for 5 minutes until the fish is just cooked through.

Sprinkle with chopped chives and serve.

Chicken

Yogurt chicken curry

Black pepper chicken

Butter chicken

Korma-style chicken curry

Malvani-style chicken sabji

Spinach chicken

Pulled tandoori-spiced chicken

Masala chicken

Egg & cabbage curry

I have shared other yogurt chicken recipes in my previous books, but this is the easiest version and one of the most delicious ways to cook chicken – and it's my kids favourite. I have to admit that I usually make this with chicken on the bone, as the bones add flavour to the curry. But it does take a bit more time to cook and I know many people prefer boneless chicken. This is a foolproof curry that works every single time, and you can enjoy it with any flatbreads or rice.

Yogurt chicken curry

Dahi murg curry

SERVES 4

200ml (7fl oz) natural yogurt

1 teaspoon salt

1 teaspoon garam masala

½ teaspoon ground turmeric

½ teaspoon chilli powder

2 garlic cloves, grated

600g (1lb 5oz) boneless, skinless chicken thighs, cut into 3cm (1¼ inch) pieces

2 tablespoons sunflower oil

1 teaspoon cumin seeds

2 tomatoes, thinly sliced

20g (¾oz) fresh coriander leaves, finely chopped

Mix the yogurt, salt, spices and garlic together in a bowl. Add the chicken pieces and turn until well coated in the marinade. Let the chicken marinate while you prepare the curry base.

Heat the oil in a pan and add the cumin seeds. Once they start to sizzle, add the tomatoes and cook over a medium heat for 5 minutes until they start to soften.

Add the marinated chicken with any excess marinade and mix well, then bring to the boil. Cover and cook over a medium to low heat for 15 minutes or until the chicken is cooked through.

Sprinkle with the coriander and serve.

When you have a chicken korma in a restaurant, it tends to be sweet, sometimes with raisins and quite pale. I am not a big fan of that style of korma and once you have tried my version you may well prefer mine, too. The simple spices used in the sauce lend the chicken a lovely warmth, while you get a beautiful creaminess from the cashews, poppy seeds and onions, resulting in a deliciously delicate curry. Serve with Spiced Layered Flatbread (see page 135), chapattis or naan, or with rice.

Korma-style chicken curry

Korma murg curry

SERVES 4

2 tablespoons sunflower oil

1 cinnamon stick, broken up into small pieces

2 onions, roughly chopped

1 green chilli, roughly chopped

2 garlic cloves, roughly chopped

2.5cm (1 inch) piece of fresh root ginger, peeled and roughly chopped

50g (1¾oz) cashew nuts

1 tablespoon white poppy seeds

100ml (3½fl oz) water

1 teaspoon salt

1 teaspoon garam masala

1 teaspoon chilli powder

200ml (7fl oz) boiling water

650g (1lb 7oz) boneless, skinless chicken thighs, cut into 5cm (2 inch) pieces

1 tablespoon double cream

20g (¾oz) fresh coriander leaves, finely chopped

Heat the oil in a pan and add the cinnamon. Once it starts to sizzle, add the onions with the green chilli and cook over a medium heat for 5 minutes until they start to colour.

Add the garlic, ginger and cashew nuts and cook over a medium heat for 5 minutes until lightly golden. Stir in the poppy seeds and then pour in the measured water.

Transfer the mixture to a blender and blitz until smooth, then return to the pan.

Stir in the salt, ground spices and measured boiling water, then add the chicken pieces. Cover and cook over a medium heat for 10 minutes until the chicken is cooked through.

Add the cream and coriander, then serve.

I love a chicken curry, and it is high up on my list of favourite comfort foods. This recipe is inspired by Malvani chicken curry, which comes from a coastal region in the south west of India, and is well worth trying. The many spices used here add aromatic warmth and chilli heat to the chicken. I like this with very little sauce, so it's ideal served with any flatbread, whether you choose the Spiced Layered Flatbread (see page 135), chapattis or naan, but feel free to serve it with rice.

Malvani-style chicken sabji

Malvani sukka murg

SERVES 4

FOR THE MASALA

1 tablespoon coriander seeds

1 tablespoon fennel seeds

1 teaspoon cumin seeds

8 black peppercorns

4 cloves

seeds of 4 green cardamoms

seeds of 1 black cardamom

1 cinnamon stick, broken up into small pieces

6 dried red chillies

1 star anise

2 tablespoons desiccated coconut

200ml (7fl oz) water

FOR THE CURRY

3 tablespoons sunflower oil

2 onions, finely chopped

1½ teaspoons salt

1 teaspoon Kashmiri chilli powder

4 boneless, skinless chicken breasts, thinly sliced

To make the masala, heat a frying pan, add all the spices and coconut and dry-roast over a low heat for 1–2 minutes until you can smell their aroma and they start to colour.

Transfer to a spice blender and blitz to a powder or use a pestle and mortar to finely grind them. Add the measured water to the spice mix and mix well to form a paste.

To make the curry, heat the oil in a pan, add the onions and cook over a low to medium heat for 6–8 minutes until lightly golden. Then stir in the spice paste and cook for a minute.

Add the salt, Kashmiri chilli powder and chicken, cover and cook for 10 minutes or until the chicken is cooked through. Uncover and cook over a high heat for a minute before serving.

Chicken curry is one of my favourites and that is one reason I enjoy experimenting and trying new approaches. Here, the chicken is marinated in a ginger and garlic mixture, in which it can be left for longer if you have time. The sauce uses mostly storecupboard spices, yet once you add the amchur (mango powder) and stir puréed spinach into the creamy curry, it turns into something extraordinary. Delicious with Tamarind and Sesame Seed Rice (see page 142), or naan or chapattis.

Spinach chicken

Saag murg

SERVES 4

600g (1lb 5oz) boneless, skinless chicken thighs, cut into 4cm (1½ inch) pieces

FOR THE MARINADE

4 tablespoons natural yogurt

2.5cm (1 inch) piece of fresh root ginger, peeled and grated

2 garlic cloves, grated

½ teaspoon salt

½ teaspoon chilli powder

FOR THE CURRY

2 tablespoons sunflower oil

1 teaspoon cumin seeds

2 onions, roughly chopped

2 tomatoes, roughly chopped

1 teaspoon garam masala

1 teaspoon chilli powder

1 teaspoon amchur (mango powder)

1 teaspoon salt

200g (7oz) spinach leaves

100ml (3½fl oz) boiling water

Mix the marinade ingredients together in a bowl. Add the chicken and turn in the marinade until well coated. Leave to marinate while you cook the curry base.

Heat the oil in a pan and add the cumin seeds. Once they start to sizzle, add the onions and cook over a medium heat for 5 minutes until they start to colour. Add the tomatoes and cook for about 5 minutes until they soften. Blitz to a paste with a hand blender or in a blender or food processor.

Return the onion paste to the pan, if necessary, and add the ground spices, salt and marinated chicken with any excess marinade. Cover and cook over a medium heat for 10 minutes or until the chicken is cooked through.

Meanwhile, put the spinach leaves into another pan and pour over the measured boiling water. Cover and leave for 2 minutes until wilted. Then blitz to a purée with a hand blender or in a blender or food processor.

Stir the puréed spinach into the chicken curry and heat through, then serve.

I love tandoori chicken, and cooking a whole chicken marinated in spices on a barbecue is the best version. But I am not one to put on a barbecue if I want a quick lunch with some tandoori-style chicken, hence this recipe. The chicken tastes incredible with all the beautiful spices, while the creamy yogurt makes it tender and moist. I would recommend you serve this on top of my Cheese and Chilli Naan (see page 137), but for a 30-minute meal, feel free to use ready-made wraps.

Pulled tandoori-spiced chicken

SERVES 4

4 wraps, to serve

FOR THE CHICKEN

2 tablespoons natural yogurt

2 garlic cloves, finely chopped

1 tablespoon tandoori masala

½ teaspoon salt

2 boneless, skinless chicken breasts, each cut into 3 or 4 strips

1 tablespoon sunflower oil

2 tablespoons salted butter, plus extra to serve

FOR THE MASALA

100ml (3½fl oz) natural yogurt

30ml (1fl oz) double cream

1 teaspoon chilli powder

1 teaspoon ground coriander

1 teaspoon ground cumin

1 teaspoon kasuri methi (dried fenugreek leaves)

FOR THE SALAD

½ cucumber, thinly sliced

1 red onion, thinly sliced

1 carrot, cut into matchsticks

½ fennel bulb, thinly sliced

1 tablespoon olive oil

juice of ½ lemon

pinch of salt

pinch of ground black pepper

For the chicken, mix the yogurt, garlic, tandoori masala and salt together in a bowl. Add the chicken strips and turn until well coated in the marinade.

Heat the oil and butter in a frying pan, add the marinated chicken and cook over a medium heat for 8 minutes until the chicken is almost cooked through.

Transfer the chicken to a chopping board and use a knife and fork to pull the chicken apart into shreds. Return the pulled chicken to the pan.

Mix all the masala ingredients together in a bowl. Add to the chicken in the pan and mix well. Cook over a medium heat for 6–8 minutes until most of the liquid has cooked off.

Meanwhile, combine all the salad ingredients in a bowl.

Heat a frying pan over a low to medium heat and heat the wraps for a few seconds on each side until soft, then spread with butter.

Divide the salad between the wraps, top with the pulled chicken, roll up the wraps and serve.

When I created this dish, I had no idea how it would turn out. But once I had tasted it, I couldn't stop eating it and since then I have been making it a lot when entertaining or cooking for friends. You can also cook it on a hot barbecue or in a hot oven for about 10 minutes until cooked through. This is flavourful enough to serve on its own, although it's great with my Ginger and Chilli Chutney (see page 158). Just make sure to cook extra; it's devilishly moreish.

Masala chicken

Masala murg

SERVES 4

50g (1¾oz) gram flour (besan/chickpea flour)

70ml (2½fl oz) natural yogurt

½ teaspoon black salt (kala namak)

1 teaspoon Kashmiri chilli powder

1 teaspoon kasuri methi (dried fenugreek leaves)

½ teaspoon garam masala

½ teaspoon ground cumin

4 boneless, skinless chicken thighs, cut into 5cm (2 inch) pieces

3 tablespoons sunflower oil

Heat a frying pan, add the flour and toast over a low heat for about 2 minutes or until it starts to change colour, stirring constantly.

Put the toasted flour into a bowl with the yogurt, salt and spices and mix together well. Add the chicken pieces and turn in the marinade until well coated.

Heat the oil in a pan. Carefully add the marinated chicken pieces to the hot oil and cook over a medium to low heat for 8–10 minutes, turning halfway through, until golden and cooked through.

You may not have expected to find a recipe for egg curry in this chapter. I've put it here because many Hindus in India (most of whom are vegetarian) consider eggs to be a form of meat. There are so many ways of making this irresistible curry and I have shared a few versions of it over the years. The addition of cabbage in this recipe gives it a lovely texture and the egg yolks contribute an extra layer of flavour to the sauce. Serve with rice or Spiced Layered Flatbread (see page 135).

Egg & cabbage curry

Anda & patta gobhi curry

SERVES 4

FOR THE CURRY

2 tablespoons rapeseed oil

2 dried bay leaves

2 onions, thinly sliced

½ hispi cabbage, about 200g (7oz), thinly sliced

1 teaspoon sugar

1 teaspoon salt

1 teaspoon chilli powder

1 teaspoon garam masala

½ teaspoon ground turmeric

200ml (7fl oz) boiling water

FOR THE EGGS

8 eggs

4 tablespoons double cream

2 tablespoons rapeseed oil

To make the curry, heat the oil in a pan, add the bay leaves and onions and cook over a high heat for about 5 minutes. Then add the cabbage and sugar and cook over a medium heat for 10 minutes until the vegetables are soft and golden. Stir in the salt and spices and cook for a minute.

While the curry is cooking, put the eggs in a pan, cover with boiling water and cook for 10 minutes. Drain, cool under cold running water and shell them. Cut the eggs in half and separate the egg whites and yolks. Mash the egg yolks with the cream in a bowl. Heat the oil in a pan and fry the egg whites for a couple of minutes until golden.

Add the mashed yolks, fried egg whites and measured boiling water to the curry. Cover and cook over a medium heat for 5 minutes until everything has come together, then serve.

Vegetable Curries & Sabji

Tamarind aubergine curry

Mixed vegetable curry

Spinach & potato sabji

Coconut okra sabji

Paneer pav bhaji

Garlicky mushroom sabji

Cumin & mango powder cauliflower pepper sabji

Carrot & pea sabji

Spinach kofta with creamy almond-onion curry

Paneer & pea masala

New potato & tomato curry

Coconut paneer tikka

Cauliflower & sugar snap pea curry

Hyderabad-style aubergine curry

Fennel potatoes

If you are an aubergine fan, then this dish is sure to become your next favourite thing. The fried aubergine picks up on the aniseed notes of the fennel and the sour kick from the tamarind, and the whole combination is just heavenly. Be careful not to taste it too much along the way, as you might have nothing left to eat at the end! Serve with some rice or paratha.

Tamarind aubergine curry

Imli baigan curry

SERVES 2

FOR THE CURRY

1 tablespoon sunflower oil

pinch of asafoetida

2 onions, thinly sliced

1 tablespoon fennel seeds

1 teaspoon chilli powder

1 teaspoon ground ginger

200ml (7fl oz) water

1 teaspoon sugar

1 teaspoon tamarind paste

FOR THE AUBERGINE

1 aubergine, cut into fingers
5–7.5cm (2–3 inches) long

¼ teaspoon salt

2–3 tablespoons sunflower oil

To prepare the aubergine, place it on a plate, sprinkle with the salt and set aside for 10 minutes.

Meanwhile, heat the oil for the curry in a pan, add the asafoetida and let it sizzle for a few seconds. Then add the onions and cook over a medium heat for 10 minutes until golden.

Heat the oil for the aubergine in a large frying pan. Pat the aubergine fingers dry, add them to the hot oil and cook over a high heat for 2 minutes until golden.

While the aubergine is cooking, heat a small frying pan, add the fennel seeds and dry-roast over a low heat for a minute. Then use a pestle and mortar to crush them.

Add the crushed fennel seeds to the onions and cook for a minute. Then stir in the ground spices and add the fried aubergine with the measured water. Cook over a low heat for 10 minutes.

Stir in the sugar and tamarind and cook over a high heat for 5 minutes until the sauce thickens, then serve.

We all have those oddments of veg in the refrigerator – a lonely carrot, some peas, the last bit of a cauliflower or half an onion. This recipe is the perfect way to use up all those vegetable leftovers. I have used three different veg here, but you can add a few other ingredients if you have them and make this curry your own. Serve it with some rice or chapattis and a nice raita like my Cucumber Raita (see page 172) for a lovely meal.

Mixed vegetable curry

Mix sabji

SERVES 4

2 tablespoons sunflower oil

1 teaspoon cumin seeds

1 teaspoon black mustard seeds

1 bay leaf

2 onions, finely chopped

1 green chilli, finely chopped

2 garlic cloves, grated

2.5cm (1 inch) piece of fresh root ginger, peeled and grated

1 teaspoon salt

1 teaspoon ground turmeric

1 teaspoon chilli powder

1 teaspoon garam masala

1 teaspoon amchur (mango powder)

½ teaspoon sugar

2 tomatoes, finely chopped

100ml (3½fl oz) boiling water

FOR THE VEGETABLES

2 tablespoons sunflower oil

½ cauliflower, cut into small florets

2 carrots, cut into small pieces

200g (7oz) fine green beans, cut into 2.5cm (1 inch) pieces

Heat the oil in a pan and add the cumin and mustard seeds and the bay leaf. Once they start to sizzle, add the chopped onions with the green chilli and cook over a medium heat for 10 minutes until golden. Then add the garlic and ginger and cook for a minute.

Meanwhile, heat the oil for the vegetables in a large frying pan. Add all of the vegetables and cook them over a medium to high heat for 8–10 minutes until lightly coloured.

Stir the salt, ground spices and sugar into the onions with the tomatoes and cook for a minute. Then add the vegetables and pour in the measured boiling water. Cover and cook over a low to medium heat for 10 minutes until the cauliflower is soft, then serve.

The subtle flavours of the spices in panch phoran – a mix of fenugreek seeds, black mustard seeds, fennel seeds, cumin seeds and nigella seeds – cooked with potatoes results in a very delicious sabji here. Along with the spinach, the potatoes also give the sabji body, making it a perfect meal just with the Cheese and Chilli Naan (see page 137) or chapattis, or serve it on the side of any curry or dal.

Spinach & potato sabji

Palak & alu sabji

SERVES 4

2 tablespoons mustard oil (or rapeseed oil)

1 tablespoon panch phoran

2 onions, thinly sliced

2 garlic cloves, grated

2.5cm (1 inch) piece of fresh root ginger, peeled and grated

500g (1lb 2oz) baby potatoes, cut into half

1 teaspoon salt

1 teaspoon ground turmeric

1 teaspoon chilli powder

1 teaspoon amchur (mango powder)

2 tomatoes, roughly chopped

30ml (2 tablespoons) water

200g (7oz) spinach leaves, chopped

Heat the oil in a pan. Once it is hot and smoky, add the panch phoran and let it sizzle for a few seconds. Add the onions and cook over a medium heat for 5 minutes until they have softened. Then add the garlic and ginger and cook for a minute.

Add the potatoes and cook over a medium heat for about 5 minutes until they and the onions have started to colour.

Stir in the salt and ground spices followed by the tomatoes and measured water. Cover and cook over a low to medium heat for 10 minutes until the potatoes are cooked through.

Add the spinach and cook over a high heat for about 2 minutes until wilted and the liquid has reduced slightly. Serve hot.

Okra is such a lovely vegetable and doesn't get enough praise. If you aren't a fan, definitely try this sabji, as chances are it will win you over. It couldn't be simpler either – just the okra combined with fresh coconut and a few spices, and you get a wonderful dish that is light and lovely served with a nice chapatti or paratha. It's great in a wrap for lunch, or as a side with Courgette Moong Dal with Tomato Tempering (see page 118) or any other dal and raita.

Coconut okra sabji

Nariyal bhindi sabji

SERVES 4

2 tablespoons sunflower oil

2 onions, thinly sliced

¾ teaspoon salt

1 teaspoon garam masala

1 teaspoon ground coriander

½ teaspoon chilli powder

½ teaspoon ground turmeric

600g (1lb 5oz) okra, cut into 2cm (¾ inch) pieces

100g (3½oz) fresh coconut, blitzed in a blender or food processor or grated

Heat the oil in a pan, add the onions and cook over a medium heat for about 10 minutes until golden. Stir in the salt and all the spices and cook for a minute.

Add the okra and coconut, cover and cook over a medium to low heat for about 10 minutes until the okra is soft.

Remove the lid and cook over a high heat for 5 minutes to crisp up slightly, then serve.

Pav bhaji is a very popular Indian street food and here I have made my own version with paneer and peppers. The list of spices might seem rather long, but you need them all to recreate the taste of the authentic pav bhaji. If you can get hold of some ready-made pav bhaji mix from an Asian supermarket or food supplier, or make some yourself to keep in store, then simply add 2½ tablespoons of that instead.

Paneer pav bhaji

SERVES 4

4 soft bread rolls or pav, split in half horizontally

2 teaspoons salted butter, plus extra to serve

finely chopped red onion and fresh coriander leaves, to serve

FOR THE BHAJI

2 tablespoons sunflower oil

2 onions, finely chopped

2 garlic cloves, grated

2.5cm (1 inch) piece of fresh root ginger, peeled and grated

1 red pepper, cored, deseeded and finely chopped

1 green pepper, cored, deseeded and finely chopped

3 tomatoes, finely chopped

2 potatoes, peeled and cut into 2.5cm (1 inch) pieces

200ml (7fl oz) boiling water

225g (8oz) paneer, grated

juice of ½ lemon

2 tablespoons salted butter

FOR THE SPICE MIX

1 teaspoon salt

1 teaspoon ground turmeric

1 teaspoon ground cumin

1 teaspoon ground coriander

1 teaspoon amchur (mango powder)

1 teaspoon chilli powder

½ teaspoon ground cinnamon

½ teaspoon ground cardamom

¼ teaspoon ground black pepper

¼ teaspoon ground cloves

To make the bhaji, heat the oil in a pan, add the onions with the garlic and ginger and cook over a high heat for 4 minutes until they start to soften. Add the peppers and cook for 4 minutes, then add the tomatoes and cook for another 4 minutes.

Meanwhile, put the potato pieces into a pan, cover with water and bring to the boil, then cook for 5 minutes until cooked through.

Drain the potatoes, add to the bhaji mixture with the salt and all the spices and pour in the measured boiling water. Mix well, then cover and cook over a medium heat for 10 minutes.

Add the paneer and use a potato masher to mash the mixture until it is mushy and well combined. Cover again and cook for a final 3 minutes. Then add the lemon juice and butter and mix well.

Meanwhile, heat a griddle pan or heavy-based frying pan, add ½ teaspoon of the butter and toast the halves of one bread roll over a medium heat until golden on both sides. Repeat with the remaining butter and rolls.

Serve the toasted rolls warm with the bhaji, topped with a little finely chopped red onion and coriander and an extra knob of butter.

I have made many different mushroom curries over the years, but I wanted to try a new approach. So I devised this mushroom sabji with tons of flavour but without a sauce so that you can scoop it up with some naan or chapattis. Using just a handful of spices and some yogurt, you really can't go wrong with this simple dish. Serve with naan or a dal such as the Yogurt Lentil Curry (see page 110).

Garlicky mushroom sabji

Lehsun mushroom sabji

SERVES 4

2 tablespoons sunflower oil
1 teaspoon fenugreek seeds
1 onion, thinly sliced
4 garlic cloves, thinly sliced
600g (1lb 5oz) chestnut mushrooms, thinly sliced
100ml (3½fl oz) natural yogurt
½ teaspoon salt
1 teaspoon ground coriander
1 teaspoon ground cumin
1 teaspoon chilli powder
handful of chives, finely chopped

Heat the oil in a pan, add the fenugreek seeds and cook over a medium to low heat for a few seconds until they start to change colour. Add the onion and cook over a medium heat for 8–10 minutes until golden. Then add the garlic and cook for a minute.

Add the mushrooms and cook over a high heat for 5 minutes, then turn the heat down to low.

Mix the yogurt, salt and ground spices together in a bowl, then add to the mushrooms and cook for a minute, stirring constantly to prevent the yogurt from splitting.

Cook over a medium heat for 10 minutes until the liquid has almost all cooked off.

Add the chives and serve.

The soft cauliflower combined with crunchy peppers and basic spices makes this a simple yet stunning sabji, great to serve with any bread or flatbread. You can also use it in a wrap for lunch or enjoy it with some dal such as Sweet and Sour Lentils (see page 112) or curry as part of a leisurely meal.

Cumin & mango powder cauliflower pepper sabji

Jeera & amchur gobhi Shimla mirch sabji

SERVES 4

2 tablespoons sunflower oil

1 teaspoon cumin seeds

1 onion, thinly sliced

1 green chilli, thinly sliced

1 teaspoon salt

1 teaspoon ground turmeric

1 teaspoon chilli powder

1 small cauliflower, cut into small florets

1 red pepper, cored, deseeded and thinly sliced

1 green pepper, cored, deseeded and thinly sliced

1 yellow pepper, cored, deseeded and thinly sliced

1 teaspoon garam masala

1 teaspoon amchur (mango powder)

Heat the oil in a pan and add the cumin seeds. Once they start to sizzle, add the onion and green chilli and cook over a medium heat for 2–3 minutes until they have softened. Then stir in the salt, turmeric and chilli powder and cook for a few seconds.

Add the cauliflower florets, cover and cook over a medium heat for 5 minutes until they start to soften.

Stir in the peppers, garam masala and amchur. Cover again and cook over a medium to low heat for 5 minutes or until the cauliflower is tender, then serve.

This recipe is cooked in many kitchens across India in the winter when carrots and peas are in season there. I remember my mum frequently preparing this dish, making the most of the juicy, sweet veg. She would make us sit on the veranda and shell the peas for her once we got back from school. Serve the sabji with Spiced Layered Flatbread (see page 135) or Cheese and Chilli Naan (see page 137).

Carrot & pea sabji

Gajar matar ki sabji

SERVES 4

2 tablespoons ghee or sunflower oil

1 teaspoon black mustard seeds

1 teaspoon cumin seeds

2.5cm (1 inch) piece of fresh root ginger, peeled and grated

500g (1lb 2oz) carrots, cut into 1cm (½ inch) pieces

½ teaspoon salt

½ teaspoon chilli powder

½ teaspoon ground cumin

½ teaspoon garam masala

200g (7oz) frozen peas

Heat the ghee or oil in a pan and add the mustard and cumin seeds. Once they start to sizzle, add the ginger and cook over a medium heat for a minute.

Add the carrots and cook over a high to medium heat for 5 minutes until they start to colour.

Stir in the salt, spices and peas, cover and cook over a low to medium heat for 10–12 minutes until the carrots have softened. Serve hot or warm.

If you are going to try just one vegetable curry from this book, then make it this one. The smooth, creamy sauce is so delicately flavoured and the crispy spinach koftas contrast so beautifully with it, even the hardcore meat-eaters will ask for seconds. Enjoy it with naan or rice.

Spinach kofta with creamy almond-onion curry

Palak kofta with badaam pyaaz curry

SERVES 4

2 tablespoons sunflower oil

250ml (9fl oz) water

100ml (3½fl oz) natural yogurt

¾ teaspoon salt

1 teaspoon chilli powder

1 teaspoon sugar

red chilli flakes, to garnish

FOR THE PASTE

1 onion, roughly chopped

1 green chilli, roughly chopped

40g (1½oz) white poppy seeds

40g (1½oz) blanched almonds

2.5cm (1 inch) fresh root ginger, peeled and roughly chopped

2 garlic cloves, roughly chopped

100ml (3½fl oz) water

FOR THE KOFTAS

1 potato, peeled and cut into 1cm (½ inch) pieces

100g (3½oz) spinach leaves, finely chopped

½ teaspoon salt

60g (2¼oz) cornflour

sunflower oil, for shallow-frying

Blitz all the paste ingredients in a blender (preferably) or a food processor until smooth. Heat the oil in a pan and add the paste with 50ml (2fl oz) of the measured water. Cover and cook over a low to medium heat for 10 minutes, stirring halfway through.

Meanwhile, make the koftas. Put the potato pieces in a pan, cover with water and bring to the boil, then cook for 5 minutes until cooked through. Drain the potato, put it into a bowl and mash with a potato masher. Add the spinach, salt and cornflour and mix well. Divide the mixture into 10–12 portions and form each into a ball about the size of a lime, then flatten them slightly.

Heat enough oil for shallow-frying in a frying pan. Line a plate with kitchen paper. Add the koftas to the hot oil and cook over a medium to high heat for 1–2 minutes until golden and crispy. Transfer to the paper-lined plate to absorb the excess oil.

Whisk the yogurt with the remaining 200ml (7fl oz) water in a small bowl. Gradually add to the paste and cook over a low heat, stirring constantly, for a minute. Then stir in the salt, chilli powder and sugar and cook for 2 minutes. Transfer to a serving bowl, place the koftas on top and serve, garnished with red chilli flakes.

Any form of paneer curry is loved in my house and this is no exception. Onions cooked with spices form the perfect flavour base for this curry, providing a lovely sauce for the paneer and peas to float in. Absolutely delicious with Cheese and Chilli Naan (see page 137) or rice, this is a crowd pleaser and such a great way to turn a midweek meal into a feast.

Paneer & pea masala

Paneer matar masala

SERVES 4

FOR THE ONION MASALA

2 tablespoons sunflower oil

2 teaspoons coriander seeds

1 teaspoon cumin seeds

1 cinnamon stick

2 cardamom pods

2 dried red chillies

2 onions, roughly chopped

1 tablespoon white poppy seeds

½ teaspoon ground turmeric

½ teaspoon salt

100ml (3½fl oz) boiling water

FOR THE CURRY

1 tablespoon ghee

1 tablespoon tomato purée

100ml (3½fl oz) boiling water

450g (1lb) paneer, cut into 2.5cm (1 inch) cubes

150g (5½oz) frozen peas

1 teaspoon salt

1 teaspoon sugar

½ teaspoon chilli powder

½ teaspoon garam masala

To make the onion masala, heat the oil in a pan and add the coriander and cumin seeds, cinnamon, cardamom and chillies. Let them sizzle for a few seconds, then add the onions and cook over a medium heat for 10 minutes until golden.

Take off the heat, add the poppy seeds, turmeric and salt and pour in the measured water. Then blitz the onion mixture to a paste in a blender (preferably) or food processor.

Heat the ghee in the same pan and add the onion masala paste and then the tomato purée. Pour in the measured boiling water and mix well, then cover and cook for 10 minutes over a medium to low heat until the tomato purée looks cooked through.

Add the remaining ingredients, cover again and cook over a medium heat for 5 minutes until everything has come together, then serve.

One for the whole family, even the fussy eaters can't say no to this simple curry. The slightly fried potatoes absorb all the amazing heat and sourness from the spices and tomatoes and become juicy and delicious. Use new potatoes in season when available, but otherwise ordinary potatoes cut into small pieces. If you have time, enjoy it with Peas-stuffed Fried Flatbread (see page 132), but it's good with rice, too.

New potato & tomato curry

Alu tamatar curry

SERVES 4

FOR THE POTATOES

2–4 tablespoons rapeseed oil

600g (1lb 5oz) new potatoes, cut in half

FOR THE CURRY

1 tablespoon rapeseed oil

pinch of asafoetida

1 teaspoon black mustard seeds

10 fresh curry leaves

1 green chilli, finely chopped

1 tablespoon sesame seeds

2.5cm (1 inch) piece of fresh root ginger, peeled and grated

4 tomatoes, finely chopped

1 teaspoon salt

1 teaspoon ground turmeric

1 teaspoon garam masala

1 teaspoon sugar

200ml (7fl oz) boiling water

juice of ½ lime

20g (¾oz) fresh coriander leaves, finely chopped

Heat the oil for the potatoes in a large frying pan. Add the potatoes, cut-side down, in a single layer and cook over a medium to high heat for 1–2 minutes until beautifully golden. You may have to do this in batches, depending on the size of your pan.

Meanwhile, start making the curry. Heat the oil in a pan and add the asafoetida. Once it starts to sizzle, add the mustard seeds with the curry leaves and chilli and cook over a low heat until they start to pop. Then add the sesame seeds and ginger and cook for a few seconds.

Add the tomatoes and cook over a medium heat for 5 minutes until they start to soften. Stir in the salt, ground spices and sugar and cook for a minute.

Add the golden potatoes and the measured boiling water, cover and cook over a low to medium heat for about 10 minutes until the potatoes are cooked through.

Add the lime juice and coriander, mix well, then serve.

I love paneer in any form – as a snack or for curries, kebabs or barbecues and even in desserts. Here, the tandoori masala marinade lends a lovely flavour to the paneer, and the many vibrant ingredients in the masala make the dish mouth-wateringly delicious. Enjoy with Spiced Layered Flatbread (see page 135) or just stuff it in a wrap for a quick lunch, or as a sabji on the side of a dal or curry.

Coconut paneer tikka

Nariyal paneer tikka

SERVES 4

FOR THE PANEER

200ml (7fl oz) natural yogurt

1 tablespoon tandoori masala

½ teaspoon salt

450g (1lb) paneer, cut into 2.5cm (1 inch) cubes

2 tablespoons sunflower oil

FOR THE MASALA

2 tablespoons sunflower oil

1 teaspoon black mustard seeds

1 tablespoon urad dal

10 fresh curry leaves

2–4 dried red chillies

3 onions, thinly sliced

60g (2¼oz) fresh coconut, grated

½ teaspoon ground turmeric

½ teaspoon chilli powder

¼ teaspoon salt

For the paneer, mix the yogurt, tandoori masala and salt together in a bowl. Add the paneer cubes and gently turn in the marinade until well coated. Set aside while you start to prepare the masala.

Heat the oil in a pan, add the mustard seeds and urad dal and cook over a low heat for a minute. Then add the curry leaves and chillies and cook for a few seconds.

Add the onions and cook over a medium heat for 10 minutes until lightly golden. Then stir in the coconut and cook for 5 minutes.

Meanwhile, heat the oil for the paneer in another pan, add the marinated paneer with all the excess marinade and cook over a high heat for 5 minutes, turning halfway through, until lovely and golden all over.

Add the cooked paneer to the onions and coconut with the turmeric, chilli powder and salt. Mix well and cook over a medium heat for 5 minutes, then serve.

Warming, light and delicious, this curry is one where you need to put in the least effort to get the best results. Once you have tried it using my suggested selection of veg, you can then vary it with different vegetables of your choice like broccoli, carrots, beans and more. This is great with Spinach Onion Pulao (see page 145) or serve with plain rice.

Cauliflower & sugar snap pea curry

Gobhi aur matar curry

SERVES 4

2 tablespoons rapeseed oil

1 teaspoon black mustard seeds

10 fresh curry leaves

1 large onion, thinly sliced

2.5cm (1 inch) piece of fresh root ginger, peeled and finely chopped

1 teaspoon salt

1 teaspoon ground turmeric

1 teaspoon chilli powder

½ teaspoon ground cinnamon

1 small cauliflower, cut into florets

1 large potato, peeled and cut into 2.5cm (1 inch) cubes

400ml (14fl oz) can coconut milk

200g (7oz) sugar snap peas

Heat the oil in a pan and add the mustard seeds. Once they start to sizzle, add the curry leaves followed by the onion and cook over a low to medium heat for 5 minutes until the onion starts to soften and colour. Then add the ginger and cook for a minute.

Add the salt and ground spices and mix well. Then add the cauliflower and potato and cook over a high heat, stirring, for 2 minutes.

Pour in the coconut milk, cover and cook over a low to medium heat for 10 minutes until the vegetables are cooked through.

Stir in the sugar snap peas and cook over a medium heat for a minute, then serve.

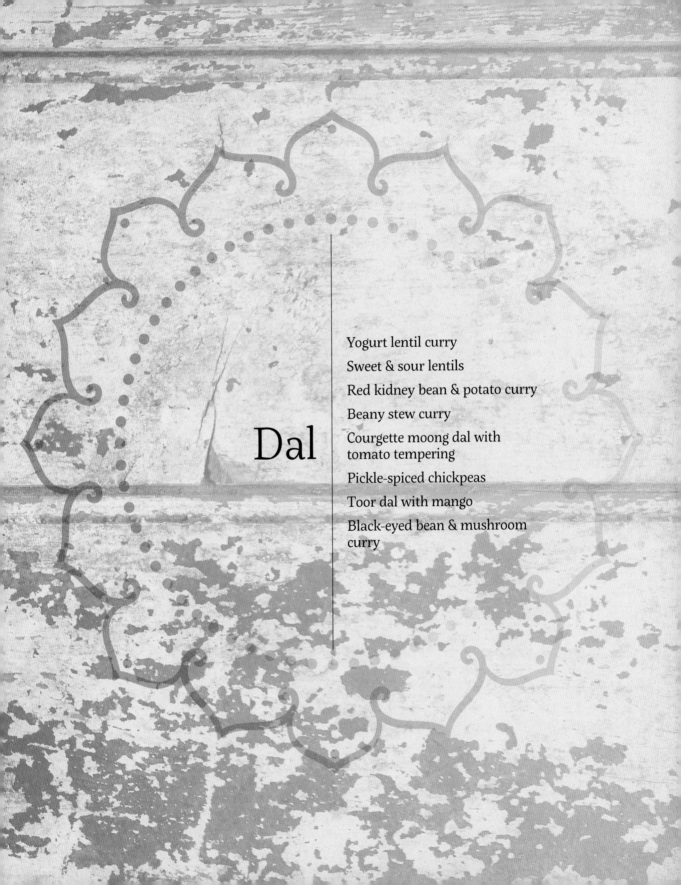

Dal

Yogurt lentil curry

Sweet & sour lentils

Red kidney bean & potato curry

Beany stew curry

Courgette moong dal with tomato tempering

Pickle-spiced chickpeas

Toor dal with mango

Black-eyed bean & mushroom curry

Sometimes all you need is just a couple of fresh ingredients thrown into a pan of simply seasoned dal to create a warming and comforting dish. The spinach along with a little yogurt makes this soothing yet deeply delicious. Serve it as a bowl of soup with some bread, or with Chicken and Potato Pulao (see page 146) or on a pile of steaming hot plain rice – the choice is yours.

Yogurt lentil curry

Dahi dal

SERVES 4

100g (3½oz) spilt moong dal

400ml (14fl oz) boiling water

½ teaspoon salt

½ teaspoon ground turmeric

2.5cm (1 inch) piece of fresh root ginger, peeled and roughly chopped

200g (7oz) spinach leaves

2 tablespoons ghee

2 onions, finely chopped

1 teaspoon chilli powder

3 tablespoons natural yogurt

Put the moong dal in a pan with the measured boiling water, salt, turmeric and ginger. Bring to the boil, then cover and cook over a low to medium heat for 10 minutes. Add the spinach, cover again and cook for another 5 minutes until the lentils are soft and the spinach has wilted.

Meanwhile, heat the ghee in a frying pan, add the onions and cook over a low to medium heat for 10 minutes until golden, then stir in the chilli powder. Remove from the heat and set aside.

Once the lentils are ready, blitz to a purée with a hand blender or in a blender or food processor. Return to the pan, if necessary, and bring to the boil. Then take off the heat, add the yogurt and mix well.

Transfer the dal to a serving bowl, top with the fried onions and serve.

Sour tamarind and sweet jaggery are a very popular traditional pairing in Indian cooking, in chutneys as well as curries and other dishes. Combining the two ingredients in this dal makes it utterly delicious. Enjoy it as a bowl of soup or serve with some piping hot rice. It's also great with Coconut Okra Sabji (see page 85).

Sweet & sour lentils

Khatti meethi dal

SERVES 4

300g (10½oz) masoor dal (split red lentils)

1 teaspoon salt

1 teaspoon ground turmeric

900ml (1½ pints) water

1 tablespoon tamarind paste

1 tablespoon jaggery, grated

FOR THE TADKA

2 tablespoons ghee

1 teaspoon black mustard seeds

10 fresh curry leaves

Put the lentils in a pan with the salt and turmeric, pour over the measured water and bring to the boil. Cover and cook over a low to medium heat for 10 minutes until the lentils are soft. Then stir in the tamarind and jaggery and cook for another minute.

To make the tadka, heat the ghee in a small pan over a medium to low heat and add the mustard seeds. Once they start to sizzle, add the curry leaves.

Pour the tadka over the cooked lentils and then serve.

I love a red kidney bean curry, or rajma as we call it, and usually soak the dried beans overnight before cooking them slowly in the curry the next day until they are super soft. Clearly, that isn't possible for a 30-minute dish, but canned beans make a good alternative, and cooked here with potato and spices, this may well become a curry favourite. Serve with rice, or Spiced Layered Flatbread (see page 135) or Tandoori Masala Roti (see page 128).

Red kidney bean & potato curry

Rajma alu

SERVES 4

2 tablespoons sunflower oil

1 teaspoon cumin seeds

10 fresh curry leaves

2 onions, finely chopped

2 garlic cloves, grated

2.5cm (1 inch) piece of fresh root ginger, peeled and grated

2 tomatoes, finely chopped

1 teaspoon salt

1 teaspoon garam masala

1 teaspoon chilli powder

1 teaspoon ground turmeric

2 teaspoons ground coriander

1 potato, peeled and cut into 1cm (½ inch) cubes

2 x 400g (14oz) cans red kidney beans, drained and rinsed

300ml (10fl oz) boiling water

handful of fresh coriander leaves

Heat the oil in a pan and add the cumin seeds and curry leaves. Once they start to sizzle, add the onions and cook over a medium heat for 6 minutes until lightly golden. Then add the garlic and ginger and cook for a minute.

Stir in the tomatoes, cover and cook over a medium heat for 5 minutes.

Add the salt and all the ground spices and mix well, then add the potato and beans with the measured boiling water. Cover and cook over a medium heat for 15 minutes, stirring halfway through. (If you have more time, you can alternatively let the curry cook over a low heat for 30–40 minutes.)

Sprinkle with the coriander leaves, then serve.

This delicious, warming, hearty stew curry featuring a combination of simple spices and beans is great for any season. Use other beans of your choice if you wish and you can also add extra herbs if you have any that need using up. This is lovely on its own or with some rice or slices of toasted sourdough.

Beany stew curry

Rajma stew curry

SERVES 4

1 tablespoon rapeseed oil

1 tablespoon salted butter

1 teaspoon cumin seeds

1 leek, trimmed, cleaned and finely chopped

2 celery sticks, finely chopped

2 garlic cloves, grated

2.5cm (1 inch) piece of fresh root ginger, peeled and finely grated

400g (14oz) can chopped tomatoes

1 teaspoon garam masala

1 teaspoon ground cumin

1 teaspoon salt

1 teaspoon chilli powder

400g (14oz) can red kidney beans, drained and rinsed

400g (14oz) can cannellini beans, drained and rinsed

400ml (14fl oz) boiling water

20g (¾oz) fresh coriander leaves, finely chopped

Heat the oil and butter in a pan and add the cumin seeds. Once they start to sizzle, add the leek and celery and cook over a medium heat for 5 minutes until softened. Then add the garlic and ginger and cook for a minute.

Pour in the tomatoes, cover and cook over a medium heat for about 5 minutes until the mixture starts to become mushy.

Stir in all the remaining ingredients except the coriander, cover again and cook over a medium to low heat for 15 minutes. (If you have more time, you can alternatively let the curry cook over a low heat for 40–45 minutes, stirring halfway through.)

Add the coriander and serve.

If you are looking for something comforting, delicious and healthy, then this dish is the perfect solution. It's a bowl of soft and mushy dal studded with golden onion and courgette, and finished with a stunning tadka of tomatoes and fresh coriander. Beautiful and satisfying on its own, it's also great served with Fennel Potatoes (see page 107), or steaming hot rice or chapattis or naan.

Courgette moong dal with tomato tempering

Moong dal with tamatar ka tadka

SERVES 4

FOR THE DAL

300g (10½oz) split moong dal

900ml (1½ pints) boiling water

1 teaspoon salt

½ teaspoon ground turmeric

2 tablespoons rapeseed oil or ghee

2 onions, finely chopped

1 courgette, thinly sliced

400ml (14fl oz) boiling water

FOR THE TADKA

1 tablespoon rapeseed oil or ghee

1 teaspoon cumin seeds

2 green chillies, thinly sliced

2 tomatoes, finely chopped

20g (¾oz) fresh coriander leaves

To make the dal, put the moong dal in a pan with the 900ml (1½ pints) measured boiling water, salt and turmeric. Bring to the boil, then cover and cook over a medium heat for 10 minutes.

Meanwhile, heat the oil or ghee in a frying pan and cook the onions and courgette over a medium heat for 7–8 minutes until golden.

Add the onions and courgette to the dal with the 400ml (14fl oz) measured boiling water, cover again and cook for another 15 minutes until the lentils are soft and mushy.

When the lentils are almost ready, make the tadka. Heat the oil or ghee in a small pan and add the cumin seeds. Once they start to sizzle, add the chillies and cook over a medium to low heat for a minute. Then add the tomatoes and cook for 5 minutes until they soften.

Once the lentils are ready, transfer to a serving bowl. Add the coriander leaves to the tadka, pour over the dal and serve.

I am a big fan of pickling spices and I like to use them in curries, as they lend them layers of flavour. If you have the time, you can use dried chickpeas here – soak in cold water overnight, drain and bring to the boil in plenty of fresh water, then simmer for about an hour or two until soft. But canned chickpeas are fine for a quick version. If you can't find or don't want to use mustard oil, use sunflower oil instead. Serve with Spiced Layered Flatbread (see page 135) or rice.

Pickle-spiced chickpeas

Aachari chole

SERVES 4

4 tablespoons mustard oil or sunflower oil

2 teaspoons fennel seeds

2 teaspoons nigella seeds

1 teaspoon black mustard seeds

1 teaspoon fenugreek seeds

1 teaspoon cumin seeds

4 dried red chillies

2 onions, finely chopped

2 garlic cloves, grated

1 teaspoon salt

1 teaspoon chilli powder

1 teaspoon ground turmeric

1 teaspoon amchur (mango powder)

1 teaspoon garam masala

1 teaspoon sugar

400g (14oz) can chopped tomatoes

2 x 400g (14oz) cans chickpeas, drained and rinsed

200ml (7fl oz) water

Heat the oil in a pan. Once it is hot and smoky, add all the spice seeds and the chillies and cook over a medium heat for a few seconds until they are all sizzling.

Add the onions and cook over a medium heat for 8 minutes until golden. Then add the garlic and cook for a minute.

Stir in all the remaining ingredients and bring to the boil. Cover and cook over a medium to low heat for 15 minutes, then serve.

For years now, I've always started the week with some kind of dal for dinner. After a weekend of overindulging it just feels right to have dal. More often than not I go for toor dal, which has a distinctive, earthy flavour. Cooking it with mango is perfect, as it gives it a sweet-sour note and also adds to the creamy texture. Serve with any sabji in the book, or with some naan or rice.

Toor dal with mango

Toor dal & aam

SERVES 2

200g (7oz) toor dal

1 litre (1¾ pints) boiling water

1 teaspoon salt

1 teaspoon ground turmeric

1 mango, preferably green (raw) or unripe ordinary mango, peeled, stoned and cut into bite-sized pieces

2 tablespoons sunflower oil or ghee

1 teaspoon cumin seeds

1 teaspoon black mustard seeds

2 green chillies, thinly sliced

1 teaspoon Kashmiri chilli powder

Put the lentils in a pan with the measured boiling water, salt, turmeric and mango. Bring to the boil, then cover and cook over a medium heat for 25 minutes until the lentils are soft.

When the lentils are almost ready, heat the oil or ghee in a small pan over a low heat and add the cumin and mustard seeds. Once they start to sizzle, stir in the chillies and chilli powder, then take the pan off the heat.

Pour over the cooked lentils and serve.

I have always loved black-eyed bean curry, a Punjabi dish made at home and enjoyed with tandoori roti back in India. Thankfully, my kids seem to enjoy it, too, which means I get to cook it often and also try different ways of combining the beans with other veg. Here, I've used mushrooms, which give an extra layer of flavour and depth to the curry. Serve with some rice or bread, such as Tandoori Masala Roti (see page 128).

Black-eyed bean & mushroom curry

Roungy mushroom curry

SERVES 4

2 tablespoons rapeseed oil

2 onions, finely chopped

2 garlic cloves, grated

2.5cm (1 inch) piece of fresh root ginger, peeled and grated

400g (14oz) can chopped tomatoes

1 teaspoon salt

1 teaspoon chilli powder

1 teaspoon garam masala

1 teaspoon ground turmeric

300g (10½oz) chestnut mushrooms, thinly sliced

400ml (14fl oz) can coconut milk

2 x 400g (14oz) cans black-eyed beans, drained and rinsed

Heat the oil in a pan, add the onions and cook over a low to medium heat for 5 minutes until softened and starting to colour. Then add the garlic and ginger and cook for a minute.

Pour in the tomatoes and cook over a low to medium heat for 5 minutes.

Stir in the salt and ground spices followed by the remaining ingredients. Mix together well and bring to the boil, then cover and cook over a medium heat for 15 minutes. (If you have more time, you can alternatively let the curry cook over a low heat for 30–40 minutes.) Serve warm.

Bread, Rice & Noodles

Tandoori masala roti

Mint & carom seed roti

Peas-stuffed fried flatbread

Spiced layered flatbread

Cauliflower-stuffed flatbread

Cheese & chilli naan

Quick uttapam

Tamarind & sesame seed rice

Spinach onion pulao

Chicken & potato pulao

Cauliflower pulao

Indian-style fried rice

Peanut & paneer rice

Upma vermicelli

Veg & egg noodles

I have some lovely memories of tandoori roti. My grandparents used to have a tandoor just outside their kitchen and every summer holiday when we went to stay there we used to have tandoori roti every day for lunch. They were some of the best lunches ever, with the whole family gathered together, and we would all wait our turn to get our roti. Coming back to this recipe, I don't have a tandoor but I make these in the oven and add the most delicious topping of all.

Tandoori masala roti

MAKES 6

FOR THE DOUGH

200g (7oz) chapatti flour, plus extra for dusting

½ teaspoon salt

2 tablespoons ghee

about 80ml (2¾fl oz) water

FOR THE TOPPING

1 onion, finely chopped

handful of fresh coriander leaves, finely chopped

1 tablespoon kasuri methi (dried fenugreek leaves)

1 teaspoon Kashmiri chilli powder

2 tablespoons ghee, plus extra to serve

Mix the flour and salt together in a bowl. Add the ghee and rub in with your fingertips until the mixture resembles breadcrumbs. Then gradually add just enough of the measured water, or a little more if needed, to bring the mixture together into a soft dough.

Knead the dough in the bowl or on a work surface for a few seconds, then cover and let it rest for 10 minutes.

Meanwhile, mix together all the topping ingredients except the ghee in a small bowl.

Preheat the grill to medium. Divide the dough into 6 portions. Roll out each portion on a lightly floured work surface to a circle or oval about 13–15cm (5–6-inches) in diameter. Spread a teaspoon of ghee on top of each, then sprinkle with one-sixth of the topping mixture and press into the dough with your fingertips. Place on a baking sheet.

Cook under the grill for a minute until golden, then turn the roti over and cook for another minute. Spread more ghee on top and serve warm.

These simple, straightforward rotis are great with any curry or as a wrap. The addition of mint and carom seeds gives them a lovely aroma and freshness. You can use only chapatti flour if you prefer, or if you can't get hold of any, replace it with wholemeal flour to go with the plain flour; either will work really well.

Mint & carom seed roti

Pudina & ajwain roti

MAKES 8

100g (3½oz) chapatti flour

100g (3½oz) plain flour, plus extra for rolling out

½ teaspoon salt

½ teaspoon carom seeds

½ teaspoon chilli powder

10g (¼oz) mint leaves, finely chopped, plus extra to garnish

about 100ml (3½fl oz) water

ghee, to serve

Mix the flours, salt, spices and mint together in a bowl. Then gradually add just enough of the measured water, or a little more if needed, to bring the mixture together into a soft dough.

Knead the dough on a work surface for a few seconds. Then return to the bowl, cover and let it rest for 5 minutes.

Divide the dough into 8 portions. Roll each in a little flour, then roll out into 10–13cm (4–5 inch) circles.

Heat a cast-iron or heavy-based frying pan over a low to medium heat. Once hot, cook one roti at a time for 1 minute on each side until golden. Spread some ghee on top and serve warm, garnished with mint leaves.

If not eating straight away, wrap up in a clean tea towel or foil to keep them soft.

For me, puris always mean feast, made on special days such as festivals and weddings and sometimes on a Sunday. They come in many different forms – plain, flavoured and also stuffed, as in this case where they are filled with lovely spiced peas. These are no less than a feast served with a chutney or just a pickle on the side, or to accompany a curry.

Peas-stuffed fried flatbread

Matar puri

MAKES 6

sunflower oil, for deep-frying

FOR THE FILLING

1 tablespoon ghee
150g (5½oz) frozen peas
1 teaspoon ground cumin
1 teaspoon chilli powder
1 teaspoon amchur (mango powder)
½ teaspoon salt

FOR THE DOUGH

75g (2¾oz) chapatti flour
75g (2¾oz) plain flour, plus extra for rolling out
1 teaspoon salt
about 90ml (6 tablespoons) water

To make the filling, heat the ghee in a pan, add the peas, spices and salt and cook over a medium heat for 5 minutes until the peas have softened. Use a potato masher to break down the peas until they are mushy.

To prepare the dough, mix the flours and salt together in a bowl. Then gradually add just enough of the measured water, or a little more if needed, to bring the mixture together into a soft dough. Knead the dough on a work surface for a few seconds. Then return to the bowl, cover and let it rest for 5 minutes.

Divide the dough into 6 portions. Roll out each portion on a work surface into a circle about 7.5cm (3 inches) in diameter. Place one-sixth of the pea filling in the centre of each circle, gather up the edges and pinch together to seal. Roll in a little flour and gently press flat with your fingertips, then roll out into 10–13cm (4–5 inch) circles.

Heat enough oil for deep-frying in a deep-fat fryer or deep, heavy-based pan (no more than one-third full) to about 170°C (340°F). Line a plate with kitchen paper. Deep-fry one puri at a time for 1–2 minutes on each side until golden brown. (Don't allow the oil to get any hotter, as they will turn golden brown on the outside before being cooked through.) Transfer to the lined plate while you fry the remaining puris. Serve warm.

People in India enjoy lachha parathas in all shapes, sizes and flavours. I often make them plain but sometimes add chaat masala for zing and kasuri methi (dried fenugreek leaves) for aroma and warmth to make them special, as here. Serve these divine parathas with any chutney in the book, or on the side of any dal or curry.

Spiced layered flatbread

Lachha paratha

MAKES 5

100g (3½oz) chapatti flour

100g (3½oz) plain flour, plus extra for rolling out

½ teaspoon salt

about 120ml (8 tablespoons) water

melted ghee or sunflower oil, for brushing and cooking

1 tablespoon chaat masala

1 tablespoon kasuri methi (dried fenugreek leaves)

Mix the flours and salt together in a bowl. Then gradually add just enough of the measured water, or a little more if needed, to bring the mixture together into a soft dough. Knead the dough in the bowl or on a work surface for a few seconds, then cover and let it rest for 5–10 minutes.

Divide the dough into 5 portions. Sprinkle each portion with flour, then roll out on a work surface into a circle about 18cm (7 inches) in diameter. Brush some ghee or oil all over each dough circle, then sprinkle with a big pinch of chaat masala and kasuri methi and gently press into the dough with your fingertips. Fold each circle into a series of pleats like a fan, then roll it up into a small roll. Sprinkle with flour, then roll out flat again into about 18cm (7 inch) circles.

Heat a heavy-based frying pan over a medium heat and cook one paratha at a time for 1 minute on each side until golden. Drizzle a teaspoon of ghee or oil over and cook for a few more seconds until crisp. Serve warm.

You can prepare and cook the parathas a few hours in advance but without adding the ghee or oil at the end, then let them cool, wrap in a clean tea towel or foil and store in an airtight container. When you are ready to eat, just reheat and crisp them up in the ghee or oil as above before serving.

I have not met anyone yet who doesn't enjoy South Indian food, especially dosa. Uttapam is made using dosa batter but is thicker and finished with different toppings. This batter usually takes a day or two to prepare, time that we might not have. So here is an instant version to satisfy your cravings for a uttapam, which you can enjoy in minutes. Serve with Coconut Chutney (see page 163) or Tomato & Tamarind Chutney (see page 166).

Quick uttapam

MAKES 6

75g (2¾oz) poha (flattened rice)
200ml (7fl oz) water
75g (2¾oz) fine semolina
110ml (3¾fl oz) natural yogurt
½ teaspoon salt
sunflower oil, for cooking

FOR THE TOPPING
1 onion, finely chopped
1 tomato, finely chopped
1 green chilli, finely chopped
good pinch of salt
good pinch of chilli powder
10g (¼oz) fresh coriander leaves, finely chopped

Soak the poha in the measured water for 5 minutes until softened.

Meanwhile, mix all the topping ingredients together in a bowl.

Drain the soaked poha, put into a blender with the semolina, yogurt and salt and blitz to a smooth batter.

Heat a frying pan over a medium heat, add a few drops of oil and then wipe out the pan. Add a ladleful of the uttapam batter and use the base of the ladle to spread it into a 13cm (5 inch) circle. Top with one-sixth of the topping mixture and drizzle ½ teaspoon of oil around the edges of the uttapam. Cook for about 2 minutes on each side until golden. Remove from the pan and repeat with the remaining batter and topping mixture. Serve warm.

The simple addition of the sour tamarind and creamy sesame is what makes this rice dish stand out from the rest. A bowlful of this warm rice is enough on its own but you can also serve it with a curry or dal, a spicy chutney or with Cheese and Chilli Naan (see page 137).

Tamarind & sesame seed rice

Imli & till ke chawal

SERVES 4

300g (10½oz) uncooked basmati rice or 900g (2lb) cooked

2 tablespoons sunflower oil

2 onions, thinly sliced

3 tablespoons white sesame seeds

2 garlic cloves, grated

2.5cm (1 inch) piece of fresh root ginger, peeled and grated

1 teaspoon salt

1 teaspoon ground turmeric

1 teaspoon chilli powder

2 tablespoons tamarind paste

1 tablespoon tahini paste

If not using previously cooked rice, wash the rice in cold water and drain, then cook in a large pan of boiling water for 8–9 minutes until tender. Drain well.

Meanwhile, heat the oil in a pan, add the onions and cook over a medium heat for 8 minutes until golden.

While the onions are cooking, heat a small pan, add the sesame seeds and dry-roast over a low heat for 1–2 minutes until lightly golden.

Add the garlic and ginger to the onions and cook for a minute. Then stir in the salt, ground spices, tamarind, tahini and 2 tablespoons of the roasted sesame seeds.

Mix in the cooked rice and cook over a high heat, stirring, for 2–3 minutes until heated through. Sprinkle the remaining tablespoon of toasted sesame seeds on top and serve.

Served piping hot (too-hot-to-eat hot) with just some plain yogurt on the side, onion pulao is one of my favourite things to eat, and one of the most comforting rice dishes. Here, I have added a couple of extra spices for heat and some spinach for more of a bite, making it the ultimate pulao. Serve with Cucumber Raita (see page 172) or Courgette Raita (see page 170), or any curry.

Spinach onion pulao

Palak pyaaz pulao

SERVES 4

2 tablespoons ghee

2 onions, thinly sliced

2 garlic cloves, finely chopped

1 tablespoon fennel seeds

4 black peppercorns

4 cloves

1¼ teaspoons salt

1 teaspoon chilli powder

200g (7oz) spinach leaves, finely chopped

250g (9oz) basmati rice, washed and drained

450ml (16fl oz) boiling water

Heat the ghee in a pan, add the onions and cook over a medium heat for 5 minutes until they start to change colour. Then add the garlic and cook for a minute.

Meanwhile, heat a frying pan, add the fennel seeds, peppercorns and cloves and dry-roast over a low heat for 1–2 minutes until you can smell their aroma and they start to colour.

Transfer to a spice grinder and blitz to a powder or use a pestle and mortar to finely grind them.

Stir the spice mix into the onions with the salt, chilli powder and spinach. Then add the rice and stir until it is well coated in the flavourings. Pour in the measured boiling water, mix well and bring to the boil, then cover and cook over a low heat for 14 minutes.

Take the pan off the heat and let the pulao rest, covered, for 5 minutes before serving.

Chicken and potatoes are commonly used together in curries and biryanis and the pairing is also perfect for a pulao. The whole spices lend their aroma and flavour to make this pulao outstanding. A complete meal on its own, this is a great dish to sit in the middle of the dinner table just with some cooling Cucumber Raita (see page 172) for company.

Chicken & potato pulao

Murg & alu pulao

SERVES 4

4 boneless, skinless chicken thighs, cut into 3cm (1¼ inch) pieces

1 potato, peeled and cut into 3cm (1¼ inch) pieces

FOR THE MARINADE

50ml (2fl oz) natural yogurt

1 teaspoon salt

1 teaspoon chilli powder

1 teaspoon garam masala

2 garlic cloves, grated

2cm (¾ inch) piece of fresh root ginger, peeled and grated

FOR THE RICE

2 tablespoons sunflower oil

4 cardamom pods

4 cloves

6 black peppercorns

1 bay leaf

1 cinnamon stick

1 teaspoon fennel seeds

1 teaspoon cumin seeds

2 onions, thinly sliced

400g (14oz) basmati rice, washed and drained

1 teaspoon salt

1 teaspoon chilli powder

1 teaspoon garam masala

800ml (1⅓ pints) boiling water

handful of fresh coriander leaves

Mix all the marinade ingredients together in a bowl. Add the chicken and potato pieces and turn until well coated in the marinade. Let them marinate while you start preparing the rice.

Heat the oil in a pan and add all the whole spices. Once they start to sizzle, add the onions and cook over a high heat for 5 minutes until they start to turn golden.

Add the marinated chicken and potato with any excess marinade and cook over a high heat for 5 minutes until the chicken starts to colour.

Stir in the rice, salt, chilli powder and garam masala and cook over a medium heat for a few seconds. Pour in the measured boiling water, add the coriander leaves and mix well. Bring to the boil, then cover and cook over a low heat for 12 minutes.

Take the pan off the heat and let the pulao rest, covered, for a few minutes before serving.

This warming, comforting cauliflower rice with some raita and chutney is a perfect plate of food for me. You can serve it warm when it's cold outside and in the summer enjoy it at room temperature with some barbecued meat or veg, making it a great recipe to cook any time of the year.

Cauliflower pulao

Gobhi pulao

SERVES 4

2 tablespoons ghee

1 star anise

1 cinnamon stick

1 bay leaf

1 mace blade

4 cardamom pods

1 large onion, thinly sliced

1 green chilli, finely chopped

2 garlic cloves, grated

2.5cm (1 inch) piece of fresh ginger, peeled and grated

1 tomato, thinly sliced

1 teaspoon salt

1 teaspoon chilli powder

1 teaspoon garam masala

½ cauliflower, cut into 5cm (2 inch) florets

20g (¾oz) fresh coriander leaves, finely chopped

300g (10½oz) basmati rice, washed and drained

500ml (18fl oz) boiling water

Heat the ghee in a pan, add all the whole spices and let them sizzle for a few seconds. Add the onion with the green chilli and cook over a medium heat for 5 minutes until it starts to colour. Then add the garlic and ginger and cook for a minute.

Add the tomato and cook for 2 minutes until it starts to soften. Then stir in the salt, ground spices and cauliflower, followed by the coriander.

Add the rice and stir until it is well coated in all the lovely flavours. Pour in the measured boiling water, mix well and bring to the boil, then cover and cook over a low heat for 14 minutes.

Take the pan off the heat and let the pulao rest, covered, for 5 minutes before serving.

Indians love Chinese food and over many years have adapted it to their tastes. Most of us find that the best way to use up leftover rice is to make it into a fried rice, and we all have our own take on it. This is how my mum makes her fried rice and it's the version I now cook for my family, who love it as much as I do. You can of course add other vegetables of your choice.

Indian-style fried rice

SERVES 4

300g (10½oz) uncooked basmati rice or 900g (2lb) cooked

2 tablespoons sunflower oil

2 garlic cloves, finely chopped

2.5cm (1 inch) piece of fresh root ginger, peeled and finely chopped

100g (3½oz) fine green beans, finely chopped

6 spring onions, finely chopped

1 red pepper, cored, deseeded and finely chopped

1 tablespoon oyster sauce

1 tablespoon chilli sauce

1 teaspoon dark soy sauce

1 teaspoon white wine vinegar

½ teaspoon salt

¼ teaspoon ground black pepper

If not using previously cooked rice, wash the rice in cold water and drain, then cook in a large pan of boiling water for 8–9 minutes until tender. Drain well.

Meanwhile, heat the oil in a pan, add the garlic and ginger and cook over a medium to low heat for a few seconds until they start to change colour. Add the beans and cook for 5 minutes. Then add the spring onions and red pepper and cook for 5 minutes.

Add all the sauces, the vinegar, salt and pepper and mix well. Mix in the cooked rice and cook over a high heat, stirring, for 2–3 minutes until heated through, then serve.

A great way to use up leftover rice, but if you don't have any, this easy recipe is worth freshly cooking rice for. The addition of paneer and chickpeas brings bite and flavour to this lovely rice dish, while the peanuts give it crunch. It's beautiful just with some yogurt, but if you have any chutney in the refrigerator, do serve it with this. It's also great with Toor Dal with Mango (see page 122).

Peanut & paneer rice

Moongfalli and paneer chawal

SERVES 4

300g (10½oz) uncooked basmati rice or 900g (2lb) cooked

2 tablespoons sunflower oil

50g (1¾oz) raw, blanched peanuts

10 fresh curry leaves

1 teaspoon black mustard seeds

3 dried red chillies

2 tomatoes, finely chopped

1½ teaspoons salt

1 teaspoon chilli powder

1 teaspoon ground turmeric

1 teaspoon garam masala

225g (8oz) paneer, cut into 2.5cm (1 inch) cubes

400g (14oz) can chickpeas, drained and rinsed

If not using previously cooked rice, wash the rice in cold water and drain, then cook in a large pan of boiling water for 8–9 minutes until tender. Drain well.

Meanwhile, heat the oil in a pan, add the peanuts and cook over a low heat for 2–3 minutes until they are golden and toasted. Then add the curry leaves, mustard seeds and red chillies and let them sizzle for a few seconds.

Add the tomatoes and cook over a medium heat for 5 minutes until they have softened. Then add the salt and ground spices followed by the paneer and chickpeas. Mix together well and cook for 2 minutes.

Mix in the cooked rice and cook over a high heat, stirring, for 2–3 minutes until heated through, then serve immediately.

This is a popular breakfast dish in India served with chai and coriander chutney, and is very similar to upma, which is made with semolina rather than vermicelli. The whole idea of this recipe is to make it quickly and enjoy it piping hot fresh from the pan, as once it cools down it gets a bit sticky. It's even easier and speedier to make these days because you can buy ready-roasted vermicelli. Try and use the small broken pieces instead of the long thin vermicelli.

Upma vermicelli

Upma-style seviya

SERVES 4

2 tablespoons sunflower oil

1 teaspoon black mustard seeds

1 teaspoon urad dal

1 teaspoon chana dal

10 fresh curry leaves

10g (¼oz) raw, blanched peanuts

2.5cm (1 inch) piece of fresh root ginger, peeled and grated

1 green chilli, finely chopped

1 onion, finely chopped

1 carrot, finely chopped

1 red pepper, cored, deseeded and finely chopped

1 green pepper, cored, deseeded and finely chopped

100g (3½oz) roasted vermicelli

800ml (1⅓ pints) boiling water

1 teaspoon salt

1 teaspoon chilli powder

1 teaspoon ground turmeric

Heat the oil in a pan, add the mustard seeds, urad dal and chana dal and cook over a low heat for a minute. Then add the curry leaves and peanuts and cook for a minute. Stir in the ginger and cook for another minute.

Add the green chilli and onion and cook for 5 minutes until the onion has softened. Then add the carrot and peppers, cover and cook over a low heat for 5 minutes until the carrot has softened.

Meanwhile, put the vermicelli into another pan, pour over the measured boiling water and cook for 5 minutes until it has softened. Drain and set aside.

Add the salt and ground spices to the vegetables followed by the drained vermicelli and stir until well combined. Cook over a medium heat for 5 minutes. Serve warm.

A family favourite, this is an easy midweek meal to share and enjoy together. The cabbage and peppers make a lovely combination with the sauces and noodles, and the eggs add extra flavour as well as nutritional value.

Veg & egg noodles

Sabji & anda noodles

SERVES 4

2 tablespoons rapeseed oil

1 onion, thinly sliced

½ hispi cabbage, about 200g (7oz), thinly sliced

1 teaspoon sugar

1 red pepper, cored, deseeded and finely chopped

1 green pepper, cored, deseeded and finely chopped

4 egg noodle nests

1 teaspoon sesame oil

1 tablespoon oyster sauce

1 tablespoon dark soy sauce

1 tablespoon light soy sauce

1 teaspoon white wine vinegar

4 large eggs

Heat the rapeseed oil in a pan, add the onion and cook over a medium heat for 4–5 minutes until softened.

Stir in the cabbage with the sugar and cook for 7–8 minutes until it has wilted and started to colour.

Add the peppers and cook for 5 minutes until they start to soften.

While the vegetables are cooking, cook the noodles according to the packet instructions. Drain and toss with the sesame oil.

Add all the sauces and vinegar to the vegetable mixture and mix together well. Toss in the noodles and cook over a high heat for 2 minutes.

Make 4 pockets in the noodle mixture and break an egg into each. Cover and cook over a medium to low heat for 6–7 minutes until the whites of the eggs are cooked but the yolks are still runny. Serve immediately.

Chutneys & Sides

Ginger & chilli chutney

Coriander peanut chutney

Coconut chutney

Tomato & tamarind chutney

Coriander-tempered hummus

Courgette raita

Potato raita

Cucumber raita

If you are a fan of hot and spicy chutneys like me, then you have come to the right recipe. There is heat from the chillies here but also a good hit of flavour, more than you would expect from the list of ingredients. I know a good chutney and this is one of the best, I promise!

Ginger & chilli chutney

Adrak and mirchi chutney

MAKES 1 SMALL BOWLFUL

2 tablespoons rapeseed oil

100g (3½oz) fresh root ginger, peeled and thinly sliced

10 dried red chillies

75–90ml (5–6 tablespoons) water

80g (2¾oz) jaggery, grated

2 tablespoons tamarind paste

¼ teaspoon salt

FOR THE TADKA

1 tablespoon rapeseed oil

2 teaspoons white sesame seeds

Heat the rapeseed oil in a pan, add the ginger and cook over a medium to low heat for 5 minutes until it starts to change colour. Then add the chillies and cook for a minute.

Transfer the ginger and chilli mixture to a blender (preferably) or food processor and blitz, adding enough of the measured water to form a paste.

Return to the pan and add the jaggery, tamarind and salt. Cook over a medium heat for 2–3 minutes until the jaggery has melted and the mixture starts to bubble up. Pour into a serving bowl.

Heat the oil for the tadka in a small pan. Add the sesame seeds and cook over a low heat for a minute or until they start to change colour, then immediately pour over the chutney. You can serve this warm, but it is much better if left to cool.

The chutney will keep in an airtight container in the refrigerator for up to 2 weeks. You can add a few more drops of water if you prefer the consistency to be a little runnier.

I have shared a coriander chutney recipe in every cookbook that I've written. This clearly illustrates how big a fan I am of this simple yet powerful little chutney and also that there are many different ways of making it. Here, the peanuts add warmth to this very refreshing mix of herbs and lemon. I have a small bowl of this chutney in the refrigerator at all times, and you will be surprised how amazingly well it goes with absolutely anything you are eating.

Coriander peanut chutney

Dhania moongphalli chutney

MAKES 1 SMALL BOWLFUL

30g (1oz) raw, blanched peanuts

1 small onion, roughly chopped

2 garlic cloves, roughly chopped

2 green chillies, roughly chopped

40g (1½oz) fresh coriander leaves

20g (¾oz) fresh mint, leaves picked (stalks discarded)

1 teaspoon sugar

½ teaspoon salt

juice of ½ lime

75ml (5 tablespoons) water

Heat a frying pan, add the peanuts and dry-roast over a low heat for 1–2 minutes until golden.

Transfer the roasted peanuts to a blender (preferably) or food processor, add all the remaining ingredients and blitz until smooth.

The chutney will keep in an airtight container in the refrigerator for 4–5 days.

I love a good coconut chutney and there are so many to choose from. This one couldn't be easier to put together and the tadka makes it sing. It's absolutely delicious with any bread or rice, or on the side of a curry, and even great to scoop up with some crisps.

Coconut chutney

Nariyal chutney

MAKES 1 SMALL BOWLFUL

FOR THE CHUTNEY

120g (4¼oz) fresh coconut, finely chopped

½ onion, roughly chopped

1cm (½ inch) piece of fresh root ginger, peeled and finely chopped

4 dried red chillies

¼ teaspoon salt

45–60ml (3–4 tablespoons) water, if needed

FOR THE TADKA

2 tablespoons sunflower oil

1 teaspoon urad dal

1 teaspoon black mustard seeds

5–6 fresh curry leaves

2 dried red chillies

½ onion, thinly sliced

Put all the chutney ingredients into a blender and blitz to a smooth paste, adding the measured water if needed to achieve the right consistency.

To make the tadka, heat the oil in a small pan, add the urad dal and cook over a low heat for a minute until it changes colour. Then add the mustard seeds, curry leaves and chillies and let them sizzle for a few seconds. Add the onion and cook over a low to medium heat for 5 minutes until it starts to colour.

Pour the tadka over the chutney and serve.

The chutney will keep in an airtight container in the refrigerator for 4–5 days. It may become too thick, in which case just add a couple of tablespoons of water to loosen it before serving.

Tomatoes make a lovely base for a chutney, especially in the summer when they are in season and beautifully ripe, sweet and packed with flavour. This is a great way to use up any extra tomatoes you might have and don't know what to do with. It's a sweet and sour chutney, with some delicate heat from the chilli powder and a pleasing sharpness from the ginger and garlic.

Tomato & tamarind chutney

Tamatar imli chutney

MAKES 1 LARGE BOWLFUL

4 tablespoons rapeseed oil

4 tomatoes, about 500g (1lb 2oz), roughly chopped

½ teaspoon ground turmeric

2 tablespoons tamarind paste

5 garlic cloves, roughly chopped

5cm (2 inch) piece of fresh root ginger, peeled and roughly chopped

1 teaspoon black mustard seeds

¼ teaspoon salt

1 teaspoon chilli powder

50g (1¾oz) jaggery, grated

Heat 2 tablespoons of the oil in a pan, add the tomatoes and cook over a high heat for 5 minutes until they start to soften. Add the turmeric and tamarind and cook over a medium heat for 2 minutes. Then add the garlic and ginger and mix well.

Transfer the mixture to a blender or food processor and blitz to a purée.

Heat the remaining oil in the pan and add the mustard seeds. Once they start to pop, add the puréed tomato mixture with the salt and chilli powder, cover and cook over a low heat for 15 minutes. Stir in the jaggery and cook for 5 minutes until it has melted.

You can serve the chutney warm, but it tastes best when left to cool. It will keep in an airtight container in the refrigerator for 8–10 days.

To me, hummus is like chutney – a few lovely ingredients blitzed together and you have a fantastic dip or an accompaniment. I have added tons of flavour to this hummus in the form of fresh coriander and a sizzling tadka. Serve with any snacks or just smooth over some flatbreads as a gorgeous spread.

Coriander-tempered hummus

Dhaniya tadka hummus

MAKES 1 SMALL BOWLFUL

FOR THE HUMMUS

400g (14oz) can chickpeas, drained and rinsed

1 garlic clove, roughly chopped

1 green chilli, roughly chopped

20g (¾oz) fresh coriander leaves

2 tablespoons tahini

½ teaspoon salt

juice of 1 lemon

60–75ml (4–5 tablespoons) water

FOR THE TADKA

2 tablespoons rapeseed oil

1 teaspoon brown mustard seeds

10g (¼oz) fresh coriander leaves

Put all the hummus ingredients in a blender or food processor and blitz until smooth. Transfer to a serving bowl.

To make the tadka, heat the oil in a small pan over a medium to low heat and add the mustard seeds. Once they start to sizzle, take the pan off the heat, add the coriander leaves and mix well. Pour over the hummus and serve.

This will keep in an airtight container in the refrigerator for 3–4 days.

The good thing about raita is that you can make it your own by adding ingredients you like, whether that's cucumber (see page 172) or potato (see opposite). I came up with this version because I love courgettes, especially when cooked with green chilli. Enjoy it with any flatbreads, rice or papads (poppadums).

Courgette raita

SERVES 4

1 tablespoon rapeseed oil

½ teaspoon cumin seeds

1 large courgette, cut into 1cm (½ inch) pieces

1 green chilli, finely chopped

200ml (7fl oz) natural yogurt

¼ teaspoon salt

¼ teaspoon ground cumin

¼ teaspoon chilli powder

30ml (2 tablespoons) water

Heat the oil in a frying pan and add the cumin seeds. Once they start to sizzle, add the courgette and green chilli and cook over a medium heat for 6–8 minutes until golden.

Meanwhile, whisk the yogurt with the salt, ground spices and measured water in a serving bowl until well combined.

Place the cooked courgette mixture on top of the yogurt mixture and serve.

This is best enjoyed fresh, but will keep in an airtight container in the refrigerator for 2–3 days.

My in-laws, who introduced me to this raita, frequently make it at home to enjoy as part of their meals. What I love about it is the bite of the soft potato combined with the cool yogurt and the spices, and the potato also makes the raita a bit more substantial. This goes brilliantly with any curry, rice or flatbreads.

Potato raita

Alu raita

SERVES 4

400g (14oz) potatoes, peeled and cut into 1–2cm (½–¾ inch) pieces

200ml (7fl oz) natural yogurt

¼ teaspoon salt

½ teaspoon chilli powder

½ teaspoon amchur (mango powder)

½ teaspoon ground cumin

1 teaspoon cumin seeds

a few mint leaves

Put the potato pieces in a pan, cover with water and bring to the boil, then cook for 5 minutes until cooked through. Drain and let them cool for 2 minutes.

Mix the yogurt, salt and ground spices together in a serving bowl until well combined. Add the potatoes and gently mix to combine.

Heat a small frying pan, add the cumin seeds and dry-roast over a low heat for a minute. Then use a pestle and mortar to crush the seeds slightly.

Sprinkle the crushed cumin over the raita with the mint leaves. Serve immediately or chill in the refrigerator before serving.

This is best enjoyed fresh, but will keep in an airtight container in the refrigerator for 2–3 days.

Yogurt plays a big role in Indian cuisine; in the north of the country or the south, everyone enjoys it in different forms. My family insist on having yogurt, too, so whether it's rice or roti, raita on the side is a must. Not only is it cooling but it also brings out the flavours of other dishes. This simple raita has just the right ingredients to make it a perfect part of any Indian meal.

Cucumber raita

Kheera raita

SERVES 4

200ml (7fl oz) natural yogurt
¼ teaspoon salt
¼ teaspoon chilli powder
¼ teaspoon ground cumin
pinch of ground black pepper
½ cucumber, finely chopped
1 firm tomato, finely chopped
1 onion, finely chopped
1 teaspoon cumin seeds

Mix the yogurt, salt and spices together in a serving bowl until well combined.

Add the cucumber, tomato and onion and mix well.

Heat a small frying pan, add the cumin seeds and dry-roast over a low heat for a minute. Then use a pestle and mortar to crush them slightly.

Sprinkle the crushed cumin over the raita and serve.

This is best enjoyed fresh.

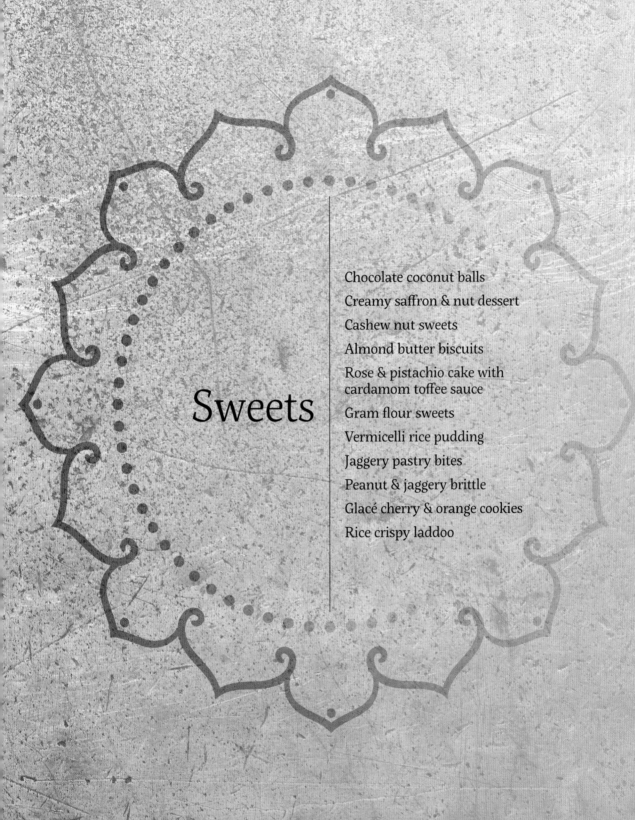

Sweets

Chocolate coconut balls

Creamy saffron & nut dessert

Cashew nut sweets

Almond butter biscuits

Rose & pistachio cake with
cardamom toffee sauce

Gram flour sweets

Vermicelli rice pudding

Jaggery pastry bites

Peanut & jaggery brittle

Glacé cherry & orange cookies

Rice crispy laddoo

These coconutty laddoos are the best little sweet ever, and so quick to prepare. My mum makes these all the time and I remember helping her to roll them out when I was growing up. I have added some chocolate to make them even more appealing for kids, and you can also roll them in chocolate sprinkles or colourful cake sprinkles instead of the pistachios if you have little people to please.

Chocolate coconut balls

Chocolate nariyal laddoo

MAKES ABOUT 12

100g (3½oz) desiccated coconut

30g (1oz) pistachio nuts

200ml (7fl oz) condensed milk

30g (1oz) 70% cocoa dark chocolate, melted

Blitz the coconut in a food processor until finely ground and set aside. Then blitz the pistachios until coarsely ground and spread out on a plate.

Heat a pan, add the coconut and cook over a low heat for 2 minutes, stirring constantly so that it doesn't colour at all.

Add the condensed milk and cook for 2 minutes, stirring constantly. Then add the melted chocolate, mix well and cook for a minute or so until the mixture starts to leave the sides of the pan and come together in a clump. Take off the heat.

Let the mixture cool slightly. Take a small portion of the mixture at a time and roll it into a walnut-sized ball, then roll in the ground pistachios to coat. Don't let the mixture cool down too much, otherwise it will be too hard to form into balls. Let the balls rest for 5 minutes and serve warm, or let them cool completely before serving.

The laddoos will keep in an airtight container in the refrigerator for 3–4 days.

This is the creamiest of desserts. The milk is cooked with condensed milk and reduced to make it thick and creamy. Each type of nut adds a different flavour note. They also soak up the milk mixture and swell up beautifully, as well as giving the dish a pleasing crunch, while the cardamom adds a lovely aromatic touch.

Creamy saffron & nut dessert

Basundi

SERVES 4

600ml (20fl oz) whole milk

pinch of saffron threads, plus extra to decorate

150ml (5fl oz) condensed milk

½ teaspoon ground cardamom

30g (1oz) cashew nuts, thinly sliced

30g (1oz) pistachio nuts, thinly sliced, plus extra to decorate

30g (1oz) almonds, thinly sliced, plus extra to decorate

Pour the milk into a pan, add the saffron and bring to the boil. Add the condensed milk and cook over a low heat for 20 minutes until the mixture has thickened and reduced slightly. You will need to stir the mixture every few minutes otherwise it will stick to the pan.

Add the cardamom and the nuts and cook over a low heat for another 5–6 minutes.

Pour the mixture into little bowls and serve warm, decorated with extra saffron, pistachios and almonds.

One of the most popular Indian sweets, these are made for special occasions like festivals, such as Diwali, and weddings. You can decorate them as you like, with silver leaf as here or with chopped nuts, or just leave them plain.

Cashew nut sweets

Kaju katli

SERVES 4

125g (4½oz) cashew nuts
1 tablespoon milk powder
½ teaspoon ground cardamom
60g (2½oz) caster sugar
30ml (2 tablespoons) water
¼ teaspoon ghee
edible silver leaf, to decorate

Blitz the cashews to a fine powder in a blender or food processor, but be careful not to overdo the blitzing to the point where the nuts release their oil. Transfer to a bowl, add the milk powder and cardamom and mix well.

Heat the sugar with the measured water in a wide pan over a low heat until it has melted. Then cook for 1 minute and no more. Keep the pan over a very low heat while you add the cashew nut mixture and stir constantly for a few seconds until the mixture starts to leave the sides of the pan and come together in a clump. Then add the ghee and mix well for a few seconds. Take off the heat.

Lay a piece of nonstick baking paper on a work surface and place the lump of hot cashew nut mixture on top. Cover with another piece of baking paper to protect your hands and knead the mixture for a few seconds. Roll it out between the sheets of baking paper to a thickness of about 3mm (⅛ inch). Let it cool for a minute, then cut into small diamond-shaped pieces.

Brush very lightly with water and place the silver leaf on top. Let the sweets cool in the refrigerator for a few minutes before serving.

The sweets will keep in an airtight container in the refrigerator for 4–5 days.

These are inspired by the butter biscuits I used to buy from the corner shop outside my college, which I thoroughly enjoyed dunking in some chai. Melting mouthfuls of buttery goodness, they are so simple to put together and the oven does the rest. You can serve them as they come, or half-dip them in melted chocolate or spread some jam on top – they are all yours to play with.

Almond butter biscuits

Badaam makhan biscuits

MAKES 20

110g (3¾oz) unsalted butter, softened

110g (3¾oz) golden caster sugar

1 teaspoon vanilla extract

150g (5½oz) ground almonds

70g (2½oz) '00' flour

handful of pistachio nuts, finely chopped

Preheat the oven to 180°C (350°F), Gas Mark 4. Line 2 baking sheets with nonstick baking paper.

Put the butter and sugar into a bowl and beat together with an electric hand mixer or by hand with a wooden spoon for a couple of minutes until pale and fluffy. Then beat in the vanilla extract.

Add the ground almonds and flour and mix until well combined.

Take small portions of the biscuit mixture and shape each portion into a ball, making 20 in total. Press gently, then place on the lined baking sheets.

Sprinkle the pistachios on top and bake for 18 minutes until lightly golden. Let them cool on the baking sheets and crisp up.

The biscuits can be kept in an airtight container for 4–5 days.

I love Indian sweets in all shapes and forms and in this recipe I wanted to bring their characteristic flavours together in the form of a cake. This subtle rose-flavoured cake made with the addition of ground pistachios is light and airy, and acts as the perfect sponge for absorbing the aromatic toffee sauce.

Rose & pistachio cake with cardamom toffee sauce

Gulab pista cake

SERVES 8

150g (5½oz) unsalted butter, softened, plus extra for greasing

150g (5½oz) golden caster sugar

150g (5½oz) self-raising flour

50g (1¾oz) ground pistachio nuts

3 eggs

½ teaspoon rose water

½ teaspoon baking powder

2 tablespoons whole milk

FOR THE TOFFEE SAUCE

50g (1¾oz) salted butter

50g (1¾oz) dark muscovado sugar

150ml (5fl oz) double cream

½ teaspoon ground cardamom

TO DECORATE

handful of pistachio nuts, roughly chopped

handful of edible dried rose petals

Preheat the oven to 180°C (350°F), Gas Mark 4. Grease and line a 20 × 30cm (8 × 12 inch) rectangular cake tin with nonstick baking paper.

Put the butter and caster sugar into a large bowl and beat together with an electric hand mixer or by hand with a wooden spoon for about a minute until pale and creamy. Alternatively, you can use a stand mixer fitted with the flat beater attachment if you have one. Add the remaining cake ingredients and beat for 2 minutes until fluffy.

Transfer the cake batter to the prepared tin and bake for 20 minutes or until a skewer inserted into the centre comes out clean.

Meanwhile, to make the toffee sauce, heat the butter and muscovado sugar together in a pan over a medium heat until the sugar has melted. Then add the cream and cardamom and bring to the boil. Let it bubble for a few seconds, then take the pan off the heat.

Once the cake is done, let it cool for 5 minutes, then turn out, remove the lining paper and place on a large serving tray. Pour the hot sauce on top, sprinkle with the pistachios and rose petals and serve.

My mum makes a few Indian sweets at home and this is one of them. She uses something called khoya (a thick milk concentrate) to make them, but since I can't get hold of any, I have started making them without it and they still taste amazing.

Gram flour sweets

Besan barfi

SERVES 8–10

100g (3½oz) ghee, plus extra for greasing

170g (6oz) gram flour (besan/chickpea flour)

60g (2¼oz) icing sugar

20g (¾oz) ground almonds

¼ teaspoon ground cardamom

10g (¼oz) toasted flaked almonds

Heat the ghee in a pan. Once it has melted, add the gram flour and cook over a low heat for 8 minutes, stirring often, until it starts to change colour and smell toasted. The mixture will start off clumpy but will gradually bubble and become smooth and creamy.

Take the pan off the heat and let the mixture cool for 5 minutes.

Meanwhile, grease a 20cm (8 inch) square cake tin and line with nonstick baking paper.

Mix the icing sugar, ground almonds and cardamom together in a bowl, then add the toasted gram flour mixture and stir to combine.

Transfer the mixture to the lined tin, then spread it out and level the surface with a spatula. Sprinkle the toasted flaked almonds on top and let it cool in the refrigerator for 5–10 minutes until firm.

Cut it into small squares and serve.

These sweets will keep in an airtight container in the refrigerator for up to 2 weeks. Let them sit at room temperature for an hour before serving.

When I was little, my grandmother used to make the dough for vermicelli and then spend hours rolling the thin noodles by hand. The noodles would then be left on big steel plates in the sun for days to dry out. My mother has now taken up making vermicelli at home and the last time she came to visit she brought me a big bagful. Vermicelli is now widely available and these days you can buy it ready-roasted, cutting another 5 minutes off your cooking time.

Vermicelli rice pudding

Seviyan kheer

SERVES 2

500ml (18fl oz) whole milk

2 tablespoons ghee

30g (1oz) cashew nuts, roughly chopped

30g (1oz) blanched almonds, roughly chopped

30g (1oz) raisins – you can use a mixture of different raisins such as black, golden and green or just one type

40g (1½oz) roasted vermicelli

40g (1½oz) light soft brown sugar

pinch of ground cardamom

Bring the milk to the boil in a pan, then take off the heat and set aside.

Heat the ghee in another pan, add the nuts and raisins and cook over a low heat for a minute until they start to change colour.

Add the vermicelli and stir well. Then gradually pour in the boiled milk and cook over a low heat for 10 minutes until the vermicelli is just soft.

Sprinkle in the sugar and cook for another 5 minutes until the milk is creamy and the vermicelli is cooked through. Then add the cardamom and mix well. Serve warm or at room temperature.

Another childhood favourite that I still enjoy when my mum visits and makes me tons. This is more of a North Indian snack, but you can find variations of these all over India. We make them with jaggery (gur), which is easily available from Asian supermarkets or food suppliers, and once you get some in stock, you can use it for other delights.

Jaggery pastry bites

Gur paare

MAKES 1 LARGE PLATEFUL

70g (2½oz) jaggery, finely chopped

45ml (3 tablespoons) water

2 tablespoons melted ghee

170g (6oz) plain flour, plus extra for dusting

sunflower oil, for deep-frying

Heat the jaggery with the measured water in a small pan over a low heat until it has melted.

Put the flour into a bowl, pour in the melted ghee and add the jaggery liquid. Mix well to form a soft dough (no kneading required).

Heat enough oil for deep-frying in a deep-fat fryer or deep, heavy-based pan (ensuring the pan is no more than one-third full) to about 150°C (300°F). Line a plate with kitchen paper.

Divide the dough into 4 portions. Roll each portion out on a lightly floured work surface to a circle about 15cm (6 inches) in diameter. Cut each circle into strips about 2.5cm (1 inch) wide and then across in the same way into small diamond shapes or squares.

Deep-fry the pastry bites, in batches, for 1–2 minutes until deep golden, stirring halfway through. (Make sure the oil is not too hot, as the pastry turns golden really quickly.) Transfer to the paper-lined plate to absorb the excess oil and cool while you fry the remaining pastry bites. They will crisp up once they have cooled down.

The pastry bites will keep in an airtight container for up to 2 weeks.

These chikkis made with jaggery are a very popular North Indian sweet prepared during the winter. There are many variations using all sorts of ingredients like sesame seeds, different nuts and puffed rice among many others, but here I've kept it simple and easy with just some roasted peanuts and jaggery.

Peanut & jaggery brittle

Moongphalli gur chikki

SERVES 6–8

180g (6¼oz) raw, blanched peanuts
sunflower oil, for oiling
1 teaspoon ghee
70g (2½oz) jaggery, grated
30ml (2 tablespoons) water

Heat a frying pan and dry-roast the peanuts over a medium heat for 3–4 minutes until golden.

Crush the roasted peanuts lightly using a pestle and mortar or enclose in a plastic bag and bash with a rolling pin.

Line a baking sheet with nonstick baking paper and brush with sunflower oil.

Heat the ghee in a pan. Once melted, add the jaggery and measured water and bring to the boil over a medium to low heat. Let the mixture bubble for a minute, then add the crushed peanuts, mix well and cook for a minute.

Spread the peanut mixture over the oiled baking paper into an even layer about 5mm (¼ inch) thick. Let it cool and set, then break it into pieces.

The brittle will keep in an airtight container for up to a week.

The tutti frutti biscuits I grew up eating back in India were the inspiration for these cookies. Since I couldn't find the tutti frutti sweets where I live, I used glacé cherries and candied peel instead, which work beautifully as chewy nuggets in these otherwise melt-in-your-mouth cookies.

Glacé cherry & orange cookies

MAKES 16

150g (5½oz) plain flour

40g (1½oz) gram flour (besan/chickpea flour)

20g (¾oz) fine semolina

70g (2½oz) icing sugar

pinch of salt

1 teaspoon ground cardamom

110g (3¾oz) ghee, melted

50g (1¾oz) glacé cherries, finely chopped

30g (1oz) mixed candied peel

Preheat the oven to 180°C (350°F), Gas Mark 4. Line 2 baking sheets with nonstick baking paper.

Mix the flours, semolina, icing sugar, salt and cardamom together in a large bowl. Add the melted ghee and mix well, then stir in the cherries and mixed peel.

Take small portions of the cookie mixture and shape each portion into a ball, making 16 in total. Place them on the lined baking sheets.

Bake for 15–18 minutes until lightly golden. Then transfer to a wire rack and let them cool and crisp up.

The cookies can be kept in an airtight container for up to a week.

This is a special little treat from my childhood that we would enjoy at winter festivals, such as on Lohri morning for breakfast. I hadn't made them for years, not since I moved to the UK, but this seemed like the perfect opportunity to share the recipe, as it's ready in minutes.

Rice crispy laddoo

Murmura laddoo

MAKES 8–10

2 tablespoons ghee
110g (3¾oz) jaggery, grated
40g (1½oz) puffed rice

Heat the ghee in a pan, add the jaggery and cook over a low heat for 4–5 minutes until it reaches 112–115°C (234–239°F) on a sugar thermometer or the soft-ball stage.

Add the puffed rice, take the pan off the heat and stir until it is all well coated in the jaggery.

Let the mixture cool for a minute or so. Then take a small portion of the mixture at a time, wrap in clingfilm, twist the ends to compact it and shape into a walnut-sized ball. Don't let the mixture cool down too much, otherwise the sugar will be too hard to form into balls, but be very careful not to burn your hands on the hot sugar and wear heat-resistant gloves if necessary. Chill the balls in the freezer for about 5 minutes until set.

These are best eaten fresh but can be kept in an airtight container for 3–4 days.

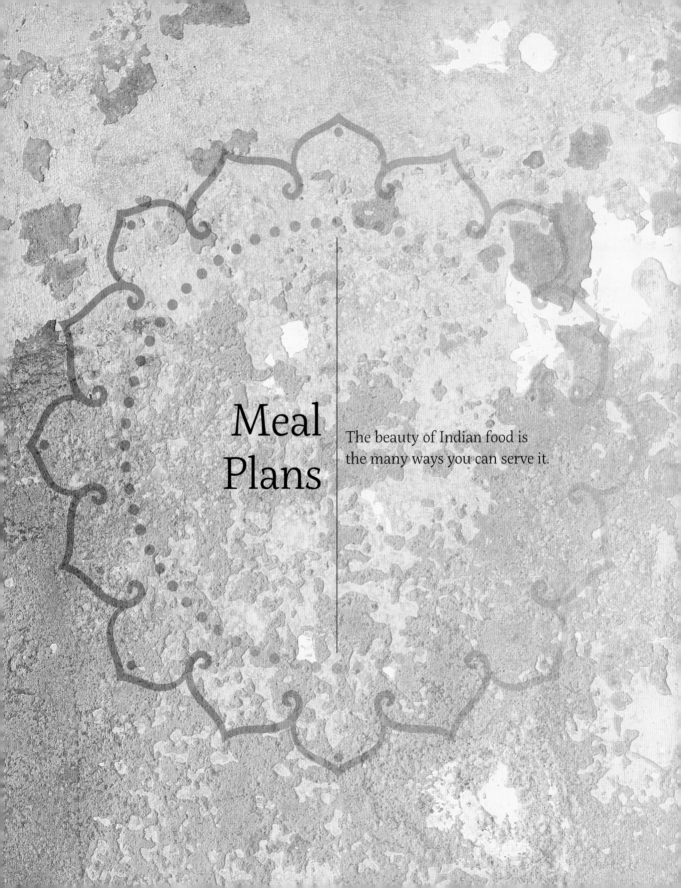

Meal
Plans

The beauty of Indian food is
the many ways you can serve it.

When it comes to your main meal, you can serve any recipe in the book with either plain rice or flatbreads, or in many cases just a piece of good toasted bread, to keep things quick and easy. But throughout the book, I have also highlighted where a specific side from another chapter goes best with a particular main dish.

There are those times, though, when you want to turn a meal into something of a feast or spread and enjoy more than one dal or curry or sabji. Choosing dishes to serve side by side where the flavours actually enhance each other is not always straightfoward, so here are some ideas of what works really well together, usually a vegetable dish or dal with a sabji or a curry and either a rice dish or flatbread. Once you have explored these meal plans as a starting point, I would encourage you to come up with your own combinations.

Coconut Paneer Tikka
(see page 103)

+

Toor Dal with Mango
(see page 122)

+

Mint & Carom Seed Roti
(see page 131)

+

Courgette Raita
(see page 170)

Masala Chicken
(see page 74)

+

Pickle-spiced Chickpeas
(see page 120)

+

Spinach Onion Pulao
(see page 145)

+

Cucumber Raita
(see page 172)

2

Malvani-style Chicken Sabji
(see page 68)

+

Mixed Vegetable Curry
(see page 82)

+

Tamarind & Sesame Seed Rice
(see page 142)

+

Cucumber Raita
(see page 172)

3

Butter Chicken
(see page 63)

+

Tamarind Aubergine Curry
(see page 80)

+

Cheese & Chilli Naan
(see page 137)

+

Potato Raita
(see page 171)

5

Spicy Tomato & Prawn Curry
(see page 55)

+

Cauliflower & Sugar Snap Pea Curry
(see page 104)

+

Tandoori Masala Roti
(see page 128)

+

Courgette Raita
(see page 170)

6

Fish & Lentil Curry
(see page 56)

+

Coconut Okra Sabji
(see page 85)

+

Quick Uttapam
(see page 140)

+

Coconut Chutney
(see page 163)

7

Carrot & Pea Sabji
(see page 94)

+

Black-eyed Bean & Mushroom Curry
(see page 123)

+

Mint & Carom Seed Roti
(see page 131)

+

Potato Raita
(see page 171)

8

New Potato & Tomato Curry
(see page 100)

+

Peas-stuffed Fried Flatbread
(see page 132)

+

Spiced Layered Flatbread
(see page 135)

+

Potato Raita
(see page 171)

11

Squid & Mangetout Curry
(see page 49)

+

Spinach & Potato Sabji
(see page 84)

+

Tandoori Masala Roti
(see page 128)

+

Cucumber Raita
(see page 172)

12

Yogurt Chicken Curry
(see page 60)

+

Sweet & Sour Lentils
(see page 112)

+

Spiced Layered Flatbread
(see page 135)

+

Potato Raita
(see page 171)

9

Korma-style Chicken Curry
(see page 67)

+

Hyderabad-style Aubergine Curry
(see page 106)

+

Spiced Layered Flatbread
(see page 135)

+

Potato Raita
(see page 171)

10

Fennel Potatoes
(see page 107)

+

Yogurt Lentil Curry
(see page 110)

+

Cauliflower-stuffed Flatbread
(see page 136)

+

Cucumber Raita
(see page 172)

13

Beany Stew Curry
(see page 115)

+

Chicken & Potato Pulao
(see page 146)

+

Coriander Peanut Chutney
(see page 162)

+

Cucumber Raita
(see page 172)

14

Amritsar-style Fish
(see page 52)

+

Red Kidney Bean & Potato Curry
(see page 114)

+

Peanut & Paneer Rice
(see page 150)

+

Cucumber Raita
(see page 172)

UK/US Glossary of Terms

aubergine......................eggplant

baking sheet..................cookie sheet

baking tray....................baking sheet

barbecue.......................grill

base..............................bottom

black-eyed beans............black-eyed peas

caster sugar...................superfine sugar

cavolo nero....................Tuscan kale

chestnut mushrooms.........cremini mushrooms

chickpeas......................garbanzo beans

chilli flakes....................red pepper flakes

chopping board...............cutting board

cling film.......................plastic wrap

coriander......................cilantro

cornflour.......................cornstarch

courgette.......................zucchini

dark chocolate................bittersweet chocolate

dark muscovado sugar.......dark brown sugar

double cream..................heavy cream

egg, medium (UK)............egg, large (US)

frying pan......................skillet

glacé cherries.................candied cherries

griddle pan....................grill pan

grill..............................broiler

hispi cabbage.................cone cabbage

icing sugar.....................confectioners' sugar

kitchen paper.................paper towels

knob of butter.................pat of butter

lengthways.....................lengthwise

light soft brown sugar.......light brown sugar

mangetout.....................snow peas

natural yogurt.................plain yogurt

nonstick baking paper.......nonstick parchment paper

pepper..........................bell pepper

plain flour......................all-purpose flour

prawns..........................shrimp

rapeseed oil....................canola oil

ready-rolled shortcrust
pastry............................pie dough sheet

self-raising flour...............self-rising flour

spring onions..................scallions

starter...........................appetizer

storecupboard.................pantry

sweets...........................candy

tea towel........................dish towel

Tenderstem broccoli..........broccolini

tin.................................pan

wholemeal flour...............whole-wheat flour

Index

Acknowledgements

With many thanks to:

My mummy and papa, for being such an inspiration in my life.

My sisters Niti and Alpa, for their constant love and support and being my top critics.

My nephew and nieces, Vanshaj, Aashvi, Reet and Reva, for making me work hard so that I can inspire them one day.

My editors, Eleanor and Louise, for always having faith in me and giving me this amazing opportunity.

Juliette and Geoff, for working so hard on the design of this book, and Leanne and Jo, for helping get the text just right.

My photographer, Nassima, who has the best eye for my food, resulting in the most beautiful pictures for this book.

Emily, for being such an amazing food stylist, and Morag, for once again creating magic with her prop styling.

Caroline and Megan, for all their support with the book promotion.

All my dear friends, who are always there with their love and support when I need it most.

This book would have not been possible without the help of my kids Sia and Yuv. They were such a big support during the lockdown and throughout the whole process of writing this book. They helped me in the kitchen, kept me on track with the schedule and really encouraged me through the whole process. They are my tasters for every single recipe that I write and never complain, although they sometimes crave just dal, rice or mac 'n' cheese, which for them is a treat after having to eat my recipes for days.

And the most important person, my husband Gaurav, who is always there for me. From listening to me talk about food and recipes all the time to being an honest taster (though I might not always take his advice on food). Without him, none of this would have been possible.